MY CAIRN CHILDREN

Mary Laurie

A Square One Publication

First published in 1995 by
Square One Publications,
The Tudor House
Upton upon Severn, Worcs WR8 2HT

© Mary Laurie 1995

British Cataloguing in Publication Date is available
for this title

My Cairn Children

ISBN 1 872017 91 6

---

*Typeset in Palatino 11 on 13 by Square One Publications,
Printed by Antony Rowe Ltd of Chippenham, England*

Also by Mary Laurie:

Single to Durban (1989)

The story of our dogs, from Jock who ruled the household for fourteen years and his little wife Buffy who died tragically, to the exuberant Susie. Interwoven is the short episode of Jessie and the story of beloved Sheena, the West Highland White, the most loving animal person I have ever known.

Sketches by C.M. Laurie

CONTENTS

INTRODUCTION

We moved into the cottage a year after the long voyage from Africa. For me, it meant coming home, back to my native East Anglia after an absence of nearly five years. Exciting years during which I had met and married Don. They say that there is a destiny that shapes our ends, and destiny had drawn me six thousand miles southwards across the oceans and brought me face to face with Don – our first casual encounter, totally unheralded and unexpected, took place on the very day I set foot in Natal. Two years later we were married.

There were three more years of ups and downs, both of us in and out of jobs, short of money and in Don's case rather short of health as well, though none of this dampened our enthusiasm in that lovely land of sunshine.

But the time came when Don lost his job again, through no fault of his own, and we had the urge to up anchor and away. We had no definite plans; I wanted him to meet my family and see my homeland, but apart from that we were content to wait and see what would turn up. So we left the fair city of Durban, our lovely flat and most of our scanty belongings, said goodbye to our friends and set sail for the UK.

And now we were settled in Suffolk, and Don was using his army training in map reading to try and find his way round the twisting by-roads of that hitherto unspoiled corner of England as a rep for a motor spares firm. There was no heater in the little Morris Minor allocated to him as a company car and he suffered badly from the cold. The first winter seemed cruel indeed, though it was nothing compared to the really record-breaking severity of the next one, in 1963.

It wasn't an old cottage – no thatched roof, or exposed beams or open fireplace and stooping doorways – just solid brick and tiles. But we loved it. It was our first real home and stood in our very own plot of land – a full third of an acre! Until then we had been flat dwellers with never as much as an open balcony where we could sit and enjoy the sun.

It stood on the site of an old sand pit, the spot selected by the gardener at the Big House of the village when his employer had offered to build him a house. The builder had engraved the date – 1915 – on the front gable.

The old gardener had enriched the sandy soil of the garden over the years, making use, no doubt, of the lavish bronze harvest that drifted down from the big oak trees every autumn, and his successors, from whom we bought it, had tended it carefully.

The cottage stood on its own, a little distance from the village. A narrow path led up to the front door; to reach the back door you had to go through a gate in the wooden fence at the side of the house and into a paved yard. There were various outbuildings; a tool shed with a honeysuckle framed window looking over the front garden, next to it a solid Anderson shelter which served as a coal shed, and on the other side of the yard a wash house, brick built with a concrete floor and a deep sink.

Behind this the garden sloped upwards, and where the steps led from a small terraced section to the top level the path was surmounted by a pergola covered with pink rambler roses. Above and beyond that the rough grassy area narrowed to a point, and a few rather stunted apple trees managed to survive in the poor sandy soil, with some lilac bushes to one side. Beyond the lilac lay the extensive vegetable garden of the next door bungalow, owned by an octogenarian widow, and over the hedge on the other side of our patch was a cornfield, and a view across farm land to the east.

Looking down from this vantage point at the top of the garden one could see across the road the low grey roof of the newly built village hall. It, too, was set in a shallow sand pit and the large area of sandy ground beside it was used as a car park. The surroundings were landscaped with shrubs, and a lot of gorse and broom had grown up. A couple of graceful silver birches, a beautiful sight in all seasons, completed the picture.

We moved in on the 7th July, a date I shall always remember. Weak from a miscarriage, I was unable to do more than supervise the placing of our few pieces of furniture and carry out the absolute minimum of cooking and cleaning. The days were long, warm and dry, and as soon as Don had departed on his day's perigrinations I would retire to the top of the garden with a deckchair. The peace and seclusion were soothing beyond words. The garden was unkempt and the grass uncut, but it was paradise to me. Woodpigeons carrooed from the oak trees, swallows burbled happily as they flitted around their nest in the woodshed. I was alone but not lonely, exulting in the sense of freedom, of knowing that there was absolutely nothing that had to be done, and all day to do it in, as the saying is.

It would be nice to have a dog. I had owned one before I left for South Africa, and Don had had an Alsatian and a Doberman Pinscer at difference times. In fact we had agreed way back in South Africa that we would need a dog. We discussed it one day over a drink as we sat in the shade outside a pub somewhere between Durban and Maritzburg, idly comparing views about the ideal home we would like to have some day. We pictured a cosy firelit scene with a dog stretched out asleep on the hearthrug - a sight unknown in the fireless houses of the semi-tropical coastline of Natal.

JOCK

He came to us a fortnight after we settled in Little Bealings. My parents and sister, who lived some twenty miles away, arrived by car, and since we had no driveway then nor parking space at the cottage, they disembarked in the grounds of the village hall just across the road, and Jock was set down on the ground. He staggered uncertainly towards us, a little straw-coloured Cairn terrier pup, just four months old. Margie had tied a narrow blue ribbon round his neck. From that moment he was our child. No meek and cuddly infant, but already a forceful little character with a mind of his own, a real personality. In fact, it was he who took possession of us and our home.

He, too, had travelled a long, long way, all the way from the Highlands of Scotland, in the care of my mother. Imprisoned in a box he was carried first on a ferry boat, then strapped to the pillion of her moped, then by train, rattling along in the guard's van across the Border and all the way down to Suffolk.

Poor Jock, he was always a bad traveller. As a puppy he could not go more than a few miles in the car before starting to dribble and then becoming really sick. That long journey from Scotland must have been a ghastly experience, and it was no wonder that he seemed wobbly on his legs when he first arrived.

From that day he was with me all day long. When I retreated to the top of the garden for a rest, he came too. He would explore the terrain all round my deck chair, pushing his way through the unmown grass, and returning from time to time to flop down and doze off beneath my chair.

11

Jock

Every day he ventured further, gradually taking possession of his territory, making his acquaintance with it inch by inch until he knew every corner, every tussock of grass and every smell in his own familiar kingdom, the garden which was to be his home for life.

At night we put him to bed in the wash house, the shed nearest the back door, in his new wicker basket. He was never left alone for long. If I had to catch the bus to go into Ipswich, though, he had to be shut in the shed. There would be temporary distress, little rattles of protest as he pawed at the door, but he would soon settle down. He did not cry or bark but accepted life philosophically.

Although he grew gradually bigger and heavier, his features did not change much over the next few weeks, and I began to think he would always have a chubby face and droopy ears. But slowly the typical Cairn features emerged. His ears pricked up and his face grew longer, so that I christened him Foxy. His first, soft puppy coat too, was gradually replaced by longer, oatmeal coloured hair.

Of course, even when he was fully grown, he was a very small dog, but he was such a character and such an important person to us that when I saw him beside Hamish, Margie's Labrador/Retriever cross, I was quite surprised to see how tiny he looked in comparison.

In his early years Jock was allowed complete freedom. The drive which was laid out soon after we arrived was open to the road, and the hedges round the garden were no barrier to a small dog. Looking back on those days, it seems incredible that we were able to leave him loose. Nowadays there is so much more through traffic, and it travels so much faster that it would be quite out of the question to let a dog roam freely on that once secluded by-road; but then we had no qualms

---

whatever. We knew that he would not stray very far, and would always return home, trotting up the front path and round to the back door in his own good time, having completed his inspection of the roadside verges, or whatever exploration he had set himself, to his own satisfaction.

When we let him out in the early morning before breakfast, his first self-imposed duty was to carefully check the scents along the grass verge on both sides of the road to see who or what had been past, then to cross to the open space in front of the village hall for a cursory inspection, and finally to trot up the drive of the bungalow next door, where there were no resident pets to look after the place, just to see that all was in order. Then he would return in a leisurely fashion and report back to the kitchen.

I loved his way of saying "hullo" when he walked into the room. It was a tiny sound like the "ow" of a feline "miaow". Long years afterwards another of my Cairn children used the same greeting.

Although he was perfectly well able to look after himself, and soon developed a good road sense, keeping close to the grass verge most of the time and moving off the road when he heard a car coming, other people seeing him on his own near the road used to get quite worried, and children would pick him up and bring him to the door. But we trusted his good sense and strong instincts, and he never came to any harm, at least not from the traffic.

I used to take him for daily walks in all directions along the country roads and footpaths and through the village to get him accustomed to walking at the side of the road, and to help him to get his bearings. Perhaps this accounts to some extent for the fact that he outlived so many of his contemporaries, some of whom, including, most tragically, his own young wife, met their death on the road. And of course he had, as we knew very well, a guardian angel incessantly watching over him.

His first taste of tragedy came when he was about six months old. He had made friends with Sweep, a black mongrel a little bigger than himself, who lived in the village. It was early November and the first really frosty night of the season. Around midnight we were woken by frantic barking from Jock, who slept in the kitchen now that the nights were getting colder. I got out of bed and hurried downstairs. Thinking there must be a feline prowler outside, which would have been enough to infuriate him, I let him out through the back door to dispatch the intruder.

Peering out through the window of the front room I caught a glimpse of two small figures flitting down the garden path and away into the shadows. The truth dawned. Sweep had come to call for his friend, and together they had gone hunting. It was a perfect night for the sport, still, clear and very cold. Calling and whistling would have been useless. So, leaving the back door closed but unlatched, so that it could be pushed open from the outside, I went back to bed.

In the morning when I went down to make the early tea I found the door half open, and there was Jock, curled up in his basket in the ice-cold kitchen. He seemed subdued, and no wonder. Driving to work a little later, Don came upon the body of Sweep, stiff and cold by the roadside just beyond the village. They had had their night's hunting – people living near the woods had heard them giving tongue during the night – and on the way home Sweep had been hit and killed by a passing car. Jock's guardian angel had done his stuff, but he was a sadder and wiser little dog. Exit friend number one.

It was a melancholy month, a season for mourning. The big

oak trees shed their leaves. On Remembrance Sunday Don got out his medals for me to polish as I polish them every year, and I shed a few tears at the sound of the Last Post. Gone are the flowers of the forest.

We went away for a couple of nights at New Year, leaving Jock in the care of a dog breeder who lived nearby. When we walked along to collect him afterwards there were several inches of snow on the ground, and he romped in ecstasy all the way home. Our elderly neighbour lent us an electric radiator for our bedroom during that cold spell, and I went to bed with a pair of slacks pulled over my pyjamas.

It was not long before friend number two came on the scene. Pip was another little Cairn terrier, so much like Jock that they were almost indistinguishable, except perhaps for Jock's slightly "gay" or curly tail. Pip was a jolly little chap and he, too, was allowed plenty of freedom. Though he lived a good mile away he often called round for a chat with Jock and a romp in the garden. There would be much nose-to-nose banter, tails wagging stiffly, and little prancing movements. Pip would stay around for just so long, then he would happily take his leave and trot off of his own accord. But sadly he, too, was to become a road casualty before he was many years older.

One of Jock's dearest friends was Dougal, a West Highland Terrier like a cuddly white bear. Their delight when they came face to face was unbounded, and they would stand on their hind legs and literally embrace. But as he grew older, Jock paid more attention to the opposite sex. In fact, it seemed at times an obsession, and led to much suffering on his part and inconvenience on ours.

His first girl friend was Smokey, an elderly cocker spaniel who lived a few hundred yards down the road towards the

Jock

village. Jock was very young at the time, but Smokey responded to his attentions with much feeling. She was very set in her ways and would not normally venture beyond her own gateway unless taken out on a lead. But now she actually appeared at the entrance to our drive one day in search of her young admirer, sniffing around a little diffidently before retreating to her own territory, Jock being indoors at the time. He soon got over his youthful infatuation.

By the following spring I was getting restless. I was not used to being a lady of leisure. Starting with a year of national service during the war I had worked all my life, apart from the years at college – not that they were times of leisure.

Housework merited only the irreducible minimum of effort, and the garden demanded little more. Without Jock's companionship and his need for daily exercise life would have been very empty; but even so I found the hours when Don was away at work too unproductive for my liking.

One weekend we drove past the research station of a well-known fertiliser company. It was an attractive low building set in immaculate turf in open countryside.

"That's where I'd like to work," I said.

Pursuing this impulse I wrote to the company and asked if there was any chance of a vacancy at the research station for a librarian, unqualified but experienced. To my surprise and delight I was very soon called for an interview. The full-time librarian was leaving, I was told, and if I found that I could do the work in the restricted hours of nine to three, as I requested, the job would be mine.

But before I could begin work there were two problems to be solved. The first was the need for transport, since a journey of eight miles was involved. This was soon solved by a visit

---

to the bank manager and the acquisition of a second-hand Austin A35.

The other problem was what to do with Jock. It was because of him that I would not consider working a full day from nine to five, but even with reduced hours he would have to be left on his own for most of the day, and this I was very reluctant to do.

Fortunately the dog breeder who had looked after him at new Year lived close by, and it was arranged that I should leave him in his care every morning, collecting him on my way home from work. His feelings about the Poodle House, as we called it in Jock's language, were rather mixed. The company was not quite what a Scotsman would choose, he felt – but it was better than solitary confinement at home.

I enjoyed the daily drive to work. Taking the shortest possible route across country involved travelling along some narrow by-ways, and was much more interesting than going by the main road. Having passed through our own small village I drove along a quiet road so overhung with trees that it seemed in places like a winding leafy tunnel, with all sunlight excluded. The beeches, oaks and sweet chestnut trees were the home of grey squirrels, occasionally to be seen flitting up the branches to vanish out of sight.

Crossing over a busy A road, I travelled next along a road skirting the perimeter fence of a disused airfield, with clumps of gorse, campion and willow herb on the airfield side and on the other a pine wood. At the further end of this road, in striking juxtaposition were outstanding symbols of ancient and modern worlds. On both sides the former heathland had been cultivated; to the left, across a cornfield was a small cluster of pines on a raised mount or tumulus, an Anglo-Saxon burial place dating back probably from the same period as the sensational burial ship that had been unearthed not so many miles away just before the war.

To the right, in stark contrast, set in the middle of another field, was a group of giant radar pylons. A pine-covered mound and a cluster of pylons – only a mile apart in space but separated by centuries of time in their origin. Then I turned into a little-used lane, so narrow that if you met another car you had to stop and possibly reverse into a gateway before you could pass. One lovely summer morning I had just entered the lane when, glancing to the right, I saw a very rare sight – rare, that is, in that part of the country. At the far side of the green cornfield, against a background of pines, was a herd of red deer basking in the early sushine. I was surprised to learn that deer still roamed the woods in those parts in spite of the increasingly busy roads and mushrooming housing developments.

The narrow lane traversed what was once the centre of a village that vanished centuries ago, almost without trace. The only dwellings remaining were a single cottage and a farmhouse set well back and half hidden by trees. But one of the farm buildings, a solid looking brick barn with flint buttresses against the walls, standng back a little from the lane on slightly higher ground, is believed to be part of what was once the village church. Perhaps the little orchard in front of it was the graveyard. The records say that in 1530 the church was "much decayed" and became unfit for divine service, and there is a rumour that it was the Black Death that destroyed the village.

The lane wound its way, narrow and treelined, until it emerged on to a wider road. One more village, then on to dual carriage way, and soon the research station came into sight. Such enviable luck was mine; the chance to enjoy a

---

fascinating daily drive followed by congenial work in the library.

Everything went smoothly until Jock's boarding arrangement broke down – the owners of the Poodle House moved away. We had to think again. For a long time we could find no solution, and poor Jock had to be left alone from half past eight until half past three every working day, an unhappy fate for a sociable little dog. Or, indeed, for any animal.

His lookout post was the sill of the front window. The piano stool was kept close to the window so that he could easily hop up on to it and thence on to the sill to take up his sentinel position. It gave him a good view of the drive and the T-junction opposite. How my conscience smote me when neighbours remarked on the forlorn little face gazing out of the window during the day. Of course, he must have slept for part of the time, but he had a very accurate built-in clock and was invariably on the lookout when I drove up to the house at half past three. Dour little Scot he might be, but I always received the warmest of tail-wagging welcomes.

Eventually I hit on an idea.

"Lonely Cairn seeks part-time hospitality while Mum is at work."

The advertisement appeared in the local paper, and at once came a heaven-sent answer. Mrs. C had no dog of her own and would gladly look after Jock during the day while her children were at school. Furthermore, her house was so close to an alternative route to work that the journey would take only a few minutes longer than at present. Her offer was accepted with alacrity, and for a long time Jock and I used to set out together in the morning; he spent the day with Mrs. C and I collected him on my way home.

It was really his fault that the scheme eventually broke

down. Mrs. C's children took pity on a stray black Labrador puppy found wandering on the common, a lanky, silky-coated fellow, already twice the size of Jock, who had apparently been abandoned by his owners. We were implored to take him in as a companion for Jock, Mr. C being averse to adopting him, and we thought we would give it a try.

With some misgivings I left Jock at home and fetched the black stray in the car. As soon as Jock set eyes on him he flew into a rage and tried to attack him. I got the poor bewildered youngster quickly into the sitting room and slammed the door to keep Jock out. While I tried to calm the visitor and work out a plan of action Jock laid seige to the room, snorting and sniffing threateningly at the door. It had only to be opened a crack for him to try and force his way in. Escaping by the other door into the hall, I telephoned Don at his office.

"Help! There's going to be bloody murder!"

I should have known better than to imagine that Jock would welcome a male companion. For some reason he particularly disliked black dogs, too, especially if they were bigger than him (and most dogs were). But now his dislike was compounded by jealous rage at the intrusion on his territory.

At last Don arrived, and without further ado the poor rejected youngster was settled in the front seat of his newly acquired sports car. It was touching to see him put his long black arms round Don's neck, as if appealing for sanctuary. Happily, Mrs. C's family relented and decided to give Rex, as he was christened, a home. Which meant, of course, that I could no longer leave Jock with her when I went to work, and we were back where we started.

I tried advertising again in the local paper for hospitality, but this time there was no response, so Jock had to resume his solitary watches.

In time I persuaded my employers to let me work from nine to one o'clock only and this was a slight improvement as far as Jock was concerned. I would arrive home at one-thirty ravenously hungry, and as soon as I had eaten we would both set out for a good long walk. It also gave me more time for my new-found interest in golf, which was a very different matter, and not at all to Jock's liking, I'm afraid. But that came later.

His second and most poignant love affair was with Sheil, a pretty little West Highland terrier who lived in the Big House across the fields. Jock used to call on her regularly, until one day he outstayed his welcome as far as her owner was concerned, and had to be driven away. He was very persistent though, and in desperation someone hurled a brick at him.

I found him huddled on the back door step in great distress, blood trickling from his mouth. I carried him indoors and he lay wheezing painfully under a chair in the sitting room until Don came home from work. Wrapping him gently in an old coat, I carried him out to the car and we drove straight to the vet's surgery, fearful that he was at his last gasp. But to our great relief the vet found no broken bones, and in a few weeks he had completely recovered.

Some time later Sheil's owner relented and telephoned us to suggest, to our great surprise, that Sheil and Jock should be mated, under supervision. The idea of crossing the two breeds was intriguing. They were more or less similar in size and in general appearance, except for colour, and Sheil's sweet docility allied to Jock's independent and highly intelligent nature should surely produce a very appealing result. There was breathtaking excitement. As I drove him to the kennels the little bridegroom was agog with anticipation, knowing very well that something wonderful was going to happen. The fulfilment of his dreams, so cruelly frustrated until now. I stayed with him during the performance, and it was arranged that we should return the next day for a repeat, "just to make sure".

Early the next morning I let him out into the garden as usual, and glancing out of the window a few minutes later I was astonished to see him sitting just inside the open door of the garage, close to my car. He had never done such a thing before; cars were things to be avoided if possible. But there he was, waiting hopefully to be taken back to the kennels to see his bride!

We counted the 63 days on the calendar. Jock was in the habit of going off on his own, and no doubt he visited Sheil from time to time. One morning he disappeared for a while, and when he returned I noticed that the usual bright, animated expression had gone from his brown eyes, replaced by an almost hurt, lustreless appearance. I was puzzled at the time, but soon forgot about it – until a couple of days later, when I heard the tragic news. Sheil had had an accident, a fall from an unfinished staircase, and had lost her puppies. Jock had discovered the truth when he went to visit her, and was grieving for her. No wonder he looked hurt. If I had not witnessed it I would not have believed his almost human reaction.

He had many other love affairs, some so intense that we had to send him away to stay at the kennels for anything up to a fortnight to keep him away from the bitch in question, for we could not keep him shut up in the house, and naturally the owners of the lady friend objected to his hanging round their premises, causing her to wail with misery and frustration. If Jock was shut up he would howl day and night in a deep, sorrowful baying tone. Once when I had enclosed him securely in the back yard, blocking the way into the garden with a length of chicken netting, he broke one of his teeth trying to gnaw through the wire. It was distressing to see and hear him.

At such times he lost a lot of weight, partly from lack of appetite in his disturbed state of mind, partly due to the frequent long excursions to try and see the current girl friend. Sometimes he would stay away all night, and we would wait anxiously for a telephone call from some irritated owner requesting us to remove him from their premises. One exasperated lady kept him shut up in her garage overnight without letting us know, while we were wondering whether he was dead or alive.

His urge to propagate the species was incredibly powerful, matched only by his craftiness in eluding us when he was so minded. Don used to leave for work later than me in the mornings, and there was more than one occasion when Jock gave him the slip and was nowhere to be found when the time came for him to be shut indoors. Once he spent nearly an hour playing hide and seek in the village with Don, making him late for an important meeting.

Perhaps we should have had him "dealt with" by the vet; it would certainly have made life a lot simpler for us.

There were not many cats in the vicinity. If ever one did appear Jock's reaction would be to try to approach it out of curiosity, ears pricked and tail wagging, but the wary animal would keep well away and soon disappear.

Occasionally to be seen stalking in the tall grass beyond the garden fence was a lean black, white and ginger patchwork female from the nearest farm. One summer I observed her coming and going from the undergrowth on the bank of the hollow road a short distance from our garden, and I discovered that she had a family of kittens hidden away in a bramble-covered nest, five tiny mewing things.

One day as I was walking past with Jock I rashly pointed them out to him, purely as a matter of interest, just as I might have said:

"Look Jock, there's a big birdie!" if I saw a seagull overhead.

His reacton was instantaneous. Instead of the tail-wagging curiosity that I had expected, his hunting instincts took over, and he fell upon the tiny kittens without a moment's hesitation, picking up each bundle in turn and nipping its neck, wiping out the entire litter in seconds. I shouted and stormed, but he took no notice whatsoever, and he was quite out of my reach.

Horrified, I felt I had to tell someone. I ran down the road and found a neighbour who came along at once with a spade and buried the little corpses in our garden beneath the oak tree.

Poor mother cat, returning to find her nest empty. Yet Jock had only obeyed his instinct and done what he thought was expected of him, with the brisk efficiency inherited from generations of his terrier clan. It would have been senseless to punish him. How was he to distinguish between the rightness or wrongness of finishing off a harmless family of kittens or a wild rabbit or rat?

When I pointed out the nest to him I had no inkling of the strength of that latent urge to destroy, though it must have been the same instinct that made him leap upon a molehill and start burrowing the instant it was brought to his attention. Hunting down and destroying vermin was in his blood.

Don had played golf in his younger days in Johannesburg, and now he was persuaded to take it up again. We both joined the nearest club, and it wasn't long before I, too, became addicted.

Apart from the game itself, one of the best things about playing was the opportunity of enjoying otherwise inaccessible countryside, away from the beaten track; the long winding fairways bordered with birch and gorse, bracken and heather. Oh, that heather, enemy of all golfers trying to play the ball from amongst its wiry stems – though the better players seem to avoid putting the ball into it in the first place.

In certain parts of the course one could hear nightngales in June, and there were woodpeckers and sand martins, and larks trebling overhead on a sunny day. Underfoot, one had to be wary of stepping on a snake in hot weather, as I did once. The young adder leapt a foot into the air and disappeared into the heather as frightened as I was myself.

Golf is a very sociable game. During the course of a round, taking three hours or more, there is bound to be a certain amount of chatter, however devout the concentration on the score, and there is the opportunity of playing with a wide cross-section of members, good, bad and indifferent players, thanks to the handicap system.

Then, back in the clubhouse, tired but exhilarated by the fresh air and exercise, there is tea and chocolate cake, or a drink at the bar, and more chatter. And always there is that powerful urge to improve one's game and reduce the handicap; wild delight at putting in a good score, gloom and doom when the card is fit only to be torn up.

An owner's preoccupation with golf can affect a dog's life very deeply. Some dogs can be trained to walk the course, to "sit" beside the tee while the players drive, to stifle the urge to go off rabbiting in the rough, and to freeze while the boss is trying to sink his putt. For such lucky dogs golf can be a joyful thing. But for others it can cast a long shadow across their lives. It can mean hours of loneliness at home or shut in the car outside the clubhouse, perhaps two or three times a week.

Jock belonged to the second category. He was disinclined to walk to heel, and if he had a mind to follow a private trail in the undergrowth he was deaf to all commands. One trial game was enough – we thought we had lost him for good when he disappeared into the bushes near the fifth tee, and it was hours before he eventually showed up again. The anxiety and embarrassment was too much.

So there was no choice but to leave him at home when we went to the club, or in the car when the weather was not too cold or too baking hot. On arrival we would let him out for a quick sniff around and then settle him inside. He would curl up on the front seat without a sound.

One day when I arrived at the club alone I let him out of the car as usual while I extricated my clubs from the boot and set up my trolley. Suddenly round the corner of the clubhouse appeared another lady member, and with her a fierce looking black and white collie. Before I could grab Jock he had leapt aggressively at the big dog, only to be tossed in the air with a squeal of pain.

I picked him up. He did not seem to be injured – apart from wounded pride – so I put him in the car and went round to the ladies' changing room to find my partner. Then we were

away to the first tee, full of pent up enthusiasm. Select a ball
– take a practice swing – and WHAM! We were off, striding
blissfully down the fairway with our trolleys in tow.

Some three hours later we limped back from the eighteenth
green to the clubhouse with considerably less alacrity. My
first action after checking my partner's card was to go to the
car to let Jock stretch his legs. He was not on the front seat
where I expected to see him, but lay curled up on the floor in
front of it, and when I opened the door and called him to
come out he made no move at first.

I soon discovered the reason. To my horror I saw that he
had a two-inch gash on his shoulder. It was not bleeding but
he was very stiff and sore. Quickly I packed up my
belongings and drove to the nearest vet. It was not normal
surgery time, and the vet was not available when we arrived.
We had an agonising wait. Jock sat uncomplaining beside my
chair in the deserted waiting room, but after half an hour of
inactivity he began to get restless. Why must we wait in that
dreadful place?

At long last the surgery door opened and we were
admitted. The patient was carefuly placed and held on the
table, and the lady vet examined him. He was found to have
had an incredibly lucky escape. The wound had exposed an
artery, but by some miracle it had not been pierced. He
submitted bravely, with none of his usual fuss, while it was
swabbed and stitched up.

In 1966 a small nest-egg, or bonsella, as they would call it in
Afrikaans, came our way, and we spent part of the money on
an extra special holiday. Leaving Jock in kennels, we sailed
from London docks on May 7th for Lisbon in the *Argentina*

Star, a small ship of the Blue Star line. It was returning unladen, and therefore unstable, to South America.

In the Bay of Biscay we encountered a Force Nine gale and were given a terrible tossing. I have never been so sick in my life. As I lay on my bed, my eyes were rivetted on my umbrella. It hung in front of me, suspended from a hook on the side of the wardrobe, and remained vertical. But the wardrobe itself, and indeed the whole stateroom, heaved continually, creaking steadily over to the right and back to the left and over and back again.

Anti-seasick pills were useless; and when the ship's doctor called to give me an injection, even he was looking strained. Don managed to stay on his feet, but reported few takers in the dining saloon, from whence came the sound of smashing crockery.

We sailed in calmer water up the Tagus, disembarked at Lisbon with great relief, and spent the night in a comfortable hotel. The next day we boarded a train and travelled unhurriedly southwards towards the Algarve. Don christened it the rock and roll railway. We rattled slowly along, passing first through what looked like paddy fields, then through uneven plots of straggling wheat, offering wonderful potential for the products of the agricultural chemical firm I worked for at home, and plantations of cork-yielding oak trees.

We stopped at every station en route. Some of the level crossing gates were operated by olive-skinned women in peasant dress, wearing the typical black headscarf under a straw hat. We were to find a refreshing honesty and cheerfulness amongst the Portugese people, in spite of apparent poverty.

The fishing villages along the Algarve were quiet and unspoilt and the hotel at Monte Gordo impeccable. We spent the long hot days mostly lying in the sun and bathing in the hotel swimming pool, too lazy to walk across the wide beach that separated the hotel premises from the sea.

It was like a second honeymoon. Somehow the big moments of my life seem to occur near the sea. I was born almost within a stone's throw of the cold, grey North Sea, and we became engaged in a timeless moment on a deserted beach in Natal. Then from my first bachelor flat, close to the south beach in Durban, I was able to enjoy a wonderful constantly changing seascape, enlivened by the sight of shipping of every kind from every part of the world coming and going from the harbour. And we spent our honeymoon – the first one, that is – at a remote hotel on the north coast of Natal, where the waves of the Indian ocean crashed unceasingly against the rocks below.

On our last day at Monte Gordo we had to be up at dawn to catch the six o'clock train to Lisbon. All through the night I had lain awake listening to the soft swish of the Atlantic wavelets gently rolling and unrolling against that perfect beach. The resultant sleepless exhaustion, coupled with the thirsty heat and the rough jolting of the train made the six and a half hour journey a nightmare. Unable to face a meal, we shared the contents of our small thermos flask filled and refilled with bitter tasting coffee to keep us going.

From Lisbon we flew back to London in a Comet, enjoying our first experience of air travel, or mine, at any rate, Don having travelled in a Lockheed Lodestar, a rather different animal, during the war.

The countryside was noticably more lush and green than when we left. I drove over to the kennels to fetch Jock. I knew that Don had given instructions for his coat to be tidied up, but it was a shock to find that he had been stripped. He

_____

looked quite pathetic. He seemed to be somehow diminished, robbed of some of his personality, and so much tinier. My reaction as he sat beside me on the front seat of the car was one of pity – "Poor little Jock, poor little Jockaboy!" I do not think it should ever be necessary to strip a Cairn.

We returned twice more to Monte Gordo, flying out to the newly opened airport at Faro. A much more convenient way to arrive, and of course incomparably quicker, but what a lot of pleasure is lost in the modern world by the hurry to get from A to B. Driving in the countryside one misses so much that could be seen and enjoyed on horseback or on a bicycle, or from a country bus, and impatient traffic tends to build up behind if one proceeds at less than the accepted speed. This seems to be determined by busy people whose only thought is to get to their destination in the shortest time possible, whereas others like to enjoy the route as they go, or at least to get a glimpse of the environment

Returning to the Algarve we found the lovely coast overrun by tourists. The same glorious expanse of beach, the same hotel, the same waiters even, but Oh dear, how worried they looked! Too many guests crammed in, children disturbing the orderly routine of the evening meal instead of dining on their own as they had previously done, the highly professional staff strained to the limit. The tiny seaside village that used to rely for its living on the sardine fishing industry was now scarred by high rise apartment blocks and an accompanying supermarket, and there was a large new hotel in the course of construction.

At the end of 1967 we had another memorable holiday, this time in Malta. Don was by now in an executive position and able to make a spur-of-the-moment decision to spend Christmas and the New Year at the newly opened Malta Hilton.

There were some magical moments. Flying over the Alps, their peaks like soft pale pink icing sugar in the late afternoon sunshine. A mass of surpliced choirboys in the hotel foyer singing carols on Christmas Eve. Waking up the next morning and looking out of our bedroom window to see a flutter of little white winged ships literally "go sailing by on Christmas Day in the Morning", a legendary carol come to life.

We enjoyed daily sessions of bridge with an Italian couple, experienced players who thrashed us well and truly – until at length in their mercy they suggested lowering the stake from six pence to one penny a hundred, at which point the tide turned and we began to win . . .

We dined with them at the Dragunara Casino, and toured part of the island in a hired car, visiting the walled city of Mdina on Boxing Day. The sky was overcast, the narrow streets deserted and quiet, and the atmosphere seemed to be charged with grim history. As we approached the ancient cathedral on foot the silence was broken by deep reverberating noonday chimes that seemed to echo from the shadows of another age.

We were shown round the beautiful interior by a Maltese guide and were slightly horrified when he pointed out an ornate half-finished tomb set aside, we were told, for a civic dignitary who was still alive and functioning. Did he ever visit his grave, I wondered, to inspect the progress?

Leaving the walled city, we went on to have lunch by the blue waters of the bay where St Paul landed after the apostolic shipwreck, and the survivors warmed themselves by a bonfire on the beach nineteen centuries ago.

Jock

There were 700 guests at the flamboyant New Year's Eve dinner dance at the hotel, but the evening was spoiled for us by the excessive cacophany produced by the bands, making conversation impossible.

Next day we took off from Luqa airport.

It was shortly after that that I began to feel uneasy. After the festivities of the last few days old habits, dreaded signs that had been dormant for years, were beginning to stir. No sooner were we airborne than Don ordered a double brandy. And soon afterwards, when the inevitable plastic meal arrived, he ordered another.

My heart sank. Sitting as I was at his right hand, I took a few sips of the obnoxious liquor, in an attempt to divert a little of what was, to him, a lethal potion. It was a wasted gesture, of course, because he simply ordered more.

However, as the journey wore on there were no obvious ill effects, no cause for embarrassment in our confined situation. It was just the seminal stage of an old familiar routine, an experience we had hoped would never be repeated.

We landed at Naples after dark, and with an hour to kill the passengers were given permission to leave the aircraft and go to the airport lounge. We climbed out. Halfway across the dimly lit expanse of tarmac that separated us from the airport buildings we were suddenly aware of a fast moving plane that had just landed and was taxying straight towards us. For a panicky second we wondered whether to turn back to our plane or run for our lives towards the lights of the airport lounge. We dashed ahead and survived.

When we finally landed at Heathrow, slushy snow was falling in the darkness.

Jock

After the feast came the reckoning. Not immediately, but little by little over the ensuing months, Don's business life was disrupted by drinking. In fact it was almost exactly a year after the holiday that he finally came to grips with the old enemy, compelled to take action.

He was on friendly terms with his GP, a kindred spirit with whom he played golf and sometimes tennis and bridge. This gentleman was fully au fait with the problem from the patient's as well as the medical point of view. Thus he was able to put Don in touch with a good psychiatrist – or trick cyclist as Don would have it – and arrange for him to go into a nursing home for a course of treatment; but not before they had been out together on an almighty binge to celebrate the end of his drinking days.

They dined out at a country hotel on a Saturday night. When Don returned at three o'clock in the morning he came upstairs, perched himself on the end of my bed, and proceeded to recount the highlights of the evening. How his companion, with his monocle in place, had attempted, successfully it seemed, to impress some Americans at the bar by letting on that he was a member of the local aristocracy; how they in turn had been impressed by "Hot Lips Henrietta", a member of the party, and further somewhat blurred anecdotes. He was fairly articulate, amazingly enough, but so drunk that he nearly toppled off the end of the bed.

On the Monday he retired voluntarily, as he had done so many times in earlier years, to the nursing home for a week of treatment, followed by several days' rest at home. After that life returned to an even keel.

I continued with my library work, Don was absorbed again with his new factory, and my diary was full of dates for golf and bridge, and "Jock to Vet", or sometimes "Jock to Kennels."

On the last day of June 1969 I made a note in the rough exercise book I call my dog diary about something quite unconnected with dogs:

Tomorrow is the investiture of the Prince of Wales at Caernarvon. It has been the sunniest June on record since 1927 according to the BBC. The temperature this afternoon must be well over 70 deg. Too hot to stay in the full sun, so I sit half in the shade of the cotoneaster growing against the old wash house, and half shaded by the washing on the line. (It won't take too long to dry today.)

Apart from the rustling of a light breeze in the high oak trees, and an occasional passing car beyond the hedge, the only sound is the ceaseless, tuneless chatter of the house sparrows, and from time to time the happy burbling of the resident swallows. In the distance there is a short-lived roar like muted thunder as an air force jet traces an arc across the sky. And by contrast, proving that this is at heart still an old-fashioned village, the voices of two elderly villagers, a man and a woman, out of sight but evidently dismounted from their bicycles and conversing earnestly with the rising inflections of the true Suffolk native.

THE COMING OF BUFFY

When Jock was going through one his fairly frequent bouts of frustrated passion we used to console him with the vague promise that "One day you shall have a little wife of your own."

The years went by and he had disappointment after disappointment. Perhaps it was unfair to have raised his hopes. But in the summer of 1969, when he was eight years old, on a sudden impulse I rang a breeder who sometimes advertised Cairn puppies for sale. Had she an adult bitch that she would be willing to sell, I enquired? It turned out that she would be passing our way the next Saturday on the way to a dog show, and was prepared to bring along a young bitch and have a preliminary discussion.

So Jock and Buffy had their first encounter. Jock made his feelings abundantly clear; in fact he would not leave her alone for a moment, sniffing delightedly, wagging his tail and tripping round and round her, in spite of the fact that she was not on heat. It was definitely love at first sight as far as he was concerned. Buffy, on her part, was interested but very coy.

She was a beautiful little dog, quite different to Jock, a red Cairn with a slightly darker brown top coat and a red-tinged undercoat, compared with his silvery wheaten hair. Her head was different, too; he had a pointed "foxy" face, hers was a trifle shorter and ever so slightly snub-nosed.

At her owner's suggestion negotiations were shelved for the time being for security reasons; our garden fences were not dog-proof and we had no garden gate to close off the drive from the road, so Jock bade Buffy a reluctant "Au revoir".

We ordered a five-bar gate for the drive and the hedges were reinforced with wire netting, and a few weeks later, on a warm Sunday afternoon, we set out to fetch her. A happy little gang of Cairns ran towards us from all corners of the garden, barking excitedly, and Buffy was handed over. She was very nervous and highly strung and rather apprehensive as we drove away, and needed a lot of reassurance and firm handling on my lap.

When we got home I stayed in the car with her on my knee while Don went to call Jock to meet her. He was so thrilled and so overcome with emotion that he nearly lost his voice. His bark became hoarse and muffled. We thought he must have laryngitis, and expected it to clear up in a few days, but in fact it was two full months before his voice returned to normal.

Buffy was accepted from the very first moment. It was lovely to watch her reactions. She had been trained for showing and breeding and was not used to being treated as a household pet. Coming from a bungalow home, too, she had never seen a staircase before – even the stairs were a novelty. And our voices must have seemed strange to her as well as our funny ways.

She was acutely sensitive to noise and would flinch at the rustle of a newspaper and shudder with fright when aircraft flew overhead. She was extremely well mannered and behaved with exemplary meekness as a young wife, yet with perfect self assurance. If Jock ever snapped at her, with a "Mind out, woman, you're in my way!", she would give as good as she got. The ritual behaviour between them was a study in dog psychology, and a source of great entertainment to us.

Jock's performance of the "bone dance" had always fascinated us. When presented with a new bone from the butcher's he would prance around it with a low triple bark of pleasure, a clearly expressed thank-you, picking it up and dropping it again and again.

When Buffy came there had to be two bones – in fact an identical pair of everything from biscuits to wicker baskets. There was a definite procedure. Each would have a good chew on their own bone, and then, by mutual consent, they would change places and each attack the other's bone.

Then there was the basket routine. Both baskets were taken into the sitting room at bedtime, and when I said goodnight they were a veritable pair of little angels – Jock usually curled up in his basket, Buffy more often than not sitting on a chair beside hers. A sweeter picture cannot be imagined. In the morning when I came down to make the tea and let them out they would return in a few minutes and without any hesitation each would curl up in the other's basket.

With Buffy for company, Jock mended his ways and ceased to roam the countryside. Though there was one occasion when he decided to take her out for a long walk. The front gate must have been left open, and the dogs were nowhere to be seen. Some time later there was a phone call from a man who lived a mile or so away to say that he had sighted both dogs near his garden. I drove there at once and was just in time to see the diminutive couple setting out side by side across the field behind the man's garden, taking a short cut home that I had often followed when walking Jock. Now he was showing Buffy the route, escorting her homewards. It was a very touching sight.

Gradually she took her place as the fourth member of our family. She was well trained and absolutely obedient, but naturally it took time for her to learn our language – and we had to learn hers, too. When Jock wanted to go outside to spend a penny he always nudged my leg with his nose, gently at first, and then more insistently if I failed to get the message. Whereas if Buffy needed to be let out she would prowl around with little mutterings until the door was opened for her.

We had been warned of the problems that would arise if we kept a dog and a bitch together, and soon we were only too painfully aware of them.

Jock's third serious accident was caused by defending his wife from an interloper. I had taken the two for a walk, leaving the gate open while we were out. But Buffy was in season at the time,and it so happened that another small neighbour called Whisky was aware of the fact, and while we were away from the premises he decided to do a recce. When we returned from our walk I closed the gate and went indoors, leaving Jock and Buffy in the garden.

Seconds later there was a furious commotion at the top of the garden. Jock and Whisky were at each other's throats, and Jock was yelping with pain as well as rage. When I had ejected Whisky I examined him. The only obvious damage was a scratch on the face. But to avoid further unpleasantness we decided to take the easy way out on that occasion and part the two while Buffy was in season, so that evening I took Jock to stay at the kennels.

He had become extremely agitated and tiresome in his attentions to Buffy, perhaps the more so since he was physically unable to make love to her. It was very sad, and we felt intensely sorry for him. At least he had been presented with a wife of his own, too late for consummation, and now having actually fought on her behalf and been injured in the process he was whisked away and banished from her presence. As I drove to the kennels he sat beside me limp with misery and frustration. I felt downright cruel.

Two days later the owner of the kennels phoned to say that he was worried about Jock's injured eye, which was showing signs of conjunctivitis. Whisky had done more damage than we thought. The vet had to be called, and there began what turned out to be weeks of painful treatment. Eventually he had to take the drastic step of cauterising the eyeball and then stitching the eyelids together to protect the eye and allow the surface to heal. For over a week poor Jock was a truly pathetic sight. Even after the stitches were removed he had to have daily treatment, and this necessitated five-mile trips to the vet's surgery at first, until we were lucky enough to find a neighbour who was sufficiently expert in handling bad tempered patients to carry out the treatment for us. Jock had to be muzzled every time, and even this operation needed great cunning and caution, for he hated to be touched if there was the slightest suspicion that more than a friendly pat was involved. He never regained the sight in his left eye, though the discharge gradually ceased.

We relied a great deal on the services of our friendly vet in those days, and he got to know Jock well. Jock, on his part, had mixed feelings about visiting the surgery and it was intriguing to watch his reactions. First, extreme reluctance to cross the threshold of the premises, with its smell of disinfectant and the strange assortment of other patients assembled and waiting – and perhaps an aura of pain? Once coaxed or dragged inside, tail wagging ever so slightly with guarded anticipation, his interest soon gave way to fright, and trembling, tail tucked in, he tried to make himself invisible behind my chair.

Twice we tried to mate him with Buffy, but without result. The second time he really was too old – he was ten by then – and physically incapable; but Oh how willing was the spirit!

Somewhat guiltily, we began to consider the possibility of mating her with another dog. A pedigree Cairn called Scampi lived a short distance away, and the proposal was put to his owner. Both dogs were taken to the kennels for the ceremony, but nothing came of it. We waited another year and tried again.

While Buffy was away at the kennels we spotted Scampi early one morning sniffing around the grassy bank beyond the garden fence. Like Buffy he was a red Cairn, and very well camouflaged against the dry grass in the background, so that only the movement gave him away. I waited for a while before letting Jock out for his early morning airing – but not long enough. Scampi reappeared immediately on the far side of the front gate, and Jock was there instantly. There was a brief nose-to-nose exchange accompanied by tail wagging at first. But it was followed by an explosion of angry snarling as Scampi announced: "I've come to see your wife, old man – where is she?"

Such a hullaballoo ensued that we had to rush out and bring the apoplectic Jock indoors, shooing Scampi away. We were surprised that Scampi knew where Buffy lived, for he was seldom walked past the house, and since she had been away at the kennels for over a week there can have been little, if any, of her scent around. But somehow he knew. We dreaded to think what problems might be in store for us when she came home again, and asked Scampi's owner to keep him away if possible – poor young lover boy. Was it fair to ask him to make love to Buffy at the kennels and then forbid him to visit her when she came home again bearing his offspring (we hoped)? And did Jock know that we had encouraged his wife to be unfaithful to him?

As her time drew near Buffy became very anxious. She burrowed into quiet corners of the house, tore up old

40

----

newspapers made available for the purpose, and her appetite became, if possible, more voracious. She always pretended she was half starving at mealtimes – now she seemed to be eating for four at least! But again there were no puppies. It was a false pregnancy.

Life returned to normal, and we ceased to watch anxiously for signs of Scampi outside the garden. He still called occasionally, but Jock was no longer disturbed when he saw him.

Our little Jockaboy, nearly twelve years old now, was becoming an old man. I quote from my dog diary:

Jan 18th 1973. Last night we felt as if we were beginning to say goodbye to him. One eye has been blind since his accident two years ago, and now the other is developing a cataract. He is getting deaf. I can stand behind him and call softly, and whereas he used to turn like a flash at the slightest whisper, I have to raise my voice now – and even then he peers the wrong way sometimes, trying to see where I am. He is getting much too fat; this has been the chief cause of his lameness. His small legs are overstrained with his weight, and his near side hind leg is wonky with arthritis. He drops asleep very quickly around the house, and has a bad wheeze. But today he is perkier, his limp less pronounced, and he was keen to walk more than the usual daily minimum distance to the far corner of the playing field (where he always performs dutifully on the headland beyond the fence). In spite of the cataract his eyes have not lost their expressiveness. He will sit quietly beside me, gazing up with a definite glow of affection and understanding when I talk to him.

The pattern of our lives had been disrupted by changes at the research station. There was reorganisation in the firm – they called it rationalisation. Heads rolled in some quarters, to coin a phrase. I had thought that my own job was quite secure, smugly confident that I gave good value for the small salary I was privileged to receive. But no. After nine years in the library I was consigned to the ranks of the army of redundant workers. It was rather shattering. I managed to find a less auspicious job with the County Council.

We debated packing our bags and returning to South Africa. We had now lived in England for over twelve years and Don had a yearning for his native land. I, too, would have loved to go back, at least for a long visit. We had almost decided to go the previous summer, and I had gone so far as to make enquiries about the costs of removal. I still have the detailed estimate from Pickfords.

But the way did not seem clear. For one thing, how could we abandon our Cairn family? The choice would lie between a long sea voyage or a shorter two-day air trip – both uncomfortable and upsetting for any animal, and especially for a highly strung and extremely sensitive dog like Buffy. The only alternative to taking them with us would have been to find a very caring adoptive home for them. With this thought in mind, it seemed like a portent when a friend volunteered to take both dogs if we did decide to go. But there was another obstacle. Don had prospered in his work and had held a managerial post for some years, but his asthma was getting worse. It had started when we were first married and had lived in the strangling humidity of the South Beach in Durban. For many years it had been a minor problem, flaring up only occasionally, mostly in damp summer conditions.

But there had been a terrifying incident the previous

summer when he woke up in the middle of the night unable to breathe. I had guided him to the open window and encouraged him to try and take in some fresh air, the worst possible action, as I learned later, for the window looked out over a field of ripe barley. I rushed downstairs to telephone the doctor – "He can't breathe, doctor, he can't even speak!"

The attack subsided gradually, leaving him weak and short of breath. As is typical with asthmatics, he suffered frequently from chest infections. It was because of such an infection that he was confined to bed on St Valentine's Day, a day I shall remember for ever. When I came home at tea time – I was by now the breadwinner for the family – one of my first actions was to put a lead on both dogs and take them out for a quick walk. We went down the road and into the deserted playing field; once inside the field I let them off their leads.

It was about 5pm and still light and there was a slight but very cold north-westerly wind. For a few minutes the dogs stayed close to me, sniffing here and there. Then from the hedge across the road came a slight rustling sound. Buffy picked it up at once. She was just coming into season, and she probably suspected it might be Scampi looking for her. Before I realised what was happening she had turned and disappeared in a flash under the gate and out on to the road.

At the same instant I heard the sond of a car coming fast along the hollow road, and the inevitable happened. A dull thump, and the car pulled up. I rushed out of the field shouting her name over and over – BUFFY! BUFFY!

She lay on the grass verge struggling slightly, her mouth half open, her brown eyes rolling and her legs twitching. There was no mess, no blood except a little trickle on her tongue. In a few minutes I was home, shouting the news up at the bedroom window to let Don know, and into the car. I laid her gently on the front seat and drove to the nearest vet, three miles away, while a passer-by took Jock home. I talked to her as I drove, telling her that everything would be all right. I hammered on the surgery door and the vet came out at once, but only to pronounce her dead. He carried her away in his arms.

My beautiful, thoroughbred, joyful little girl, always so happy – even when she was shouting, enraged, through the fence at her next door neighbour. So perfectly mannered that nothing would induce her to pass through the door in front of me unless I told her to do so. So loving, smiling and showing her teeth with a happy grin when she was being groomed, or when she lay indulged in luxury on my bed. If we went out for the evening I used to say:

"You may sleep on my bed if you like!" And when we returned she would be curled up, silky and cuddly on the bedspread. Always glad to jump lightly onto my lap when invited, always observing correct protocol with her husband, letting him have the first taste of any morsel. My little shadow, my Buffaly, my precious one. My little bedtime angel.

That night Jock was alone at bedtime, though Buffy was surely there in spirit. I kept waking in the night, seeing her lying by the road with blood on her tongue. I grieved for her for days, and had the half-conscious conviction that she was still clinging to me, and that in some way by constantly calling to her in my mind I was easing her away from this world, helping her on her way.

Some may think that a dog has no soul, but I know otherwise. Some say that dogs only appear to love us because they need us. Neither Jock nor Buffy was demonstrative, but they were certainly loving. And our next child, Sheena, was the most loving animal person I have ever known.

SHEENA

Long years ago, before I went to Africa, I had dreamt of her.
I had the clear impression of nursing in my arms a small
white dog who could neither see nor hear, and that is the
way it turned out in the end, or very nearly so.

She came to us the second day after Buffy's tragic accident,
pressed upon us, for she needed a home urgently. Margie
brought her to us in her car with some difficulty, for she was
highly excitable and only one year old, a pure bred West
Highland White. My sister stood in the front porch holding
on to the lead while this small white creature danced round
and round, never still for a minute.

She was very slender, with distinctive features: a very
slightly aquiline profile, narrow ears and slim legs – possibly
due to underfeeding as a pup.

From the very first she showed herself quite different in
temperament to the other two. She was bright and forceful,
not content to sit back and wait for attention, but every so
often coming forward exuberantly, wanting to jump on to my
lap, though she would always ask permission first. Then,
after a cuddle, her batteries recharged with affection, she
would spring upon her rubber dolly and play with it
vigorously, even fiercely. Her dolly had come with her from
her previous home in a plastic bag – or rather, her dolly's
head, for that was all that was left of it. It had a pretty face
and lots of reddish hair at first, gradually losing it over the
next dozen years, and the eyes too were only very slowly
washed off in spite of fierce licking. She was a great licker.
She licked her dolly for hours on end, and would have licked

my face if I had let her. Jock and Buffy had only ever licked my hand, no more. Another thing I noticed was her deep bark, contrasting to the shriller tone of the Cairns.

Jock grieved for Buffy at first. I sat and talked to him the evening she died, and we agreed that we would never ever forget her. I told him that she wasn't coming back any more, and no doubt he understood, for he had seen her after the accident. But he would have nothing to do with Sheena at first, understandably, and we had to keep her in the spare bedroom. I was with Jock in the sitting room one day when Sheena came downstairs into the hall, and through the closed door we heard the patter of her feet on the linoleum. For a fraction of a second Jock's eyes lit up and he looked questioningly at me – had Buffy come back after all?

Poor Sheena. For the first night she slept in our bedroom – or spent some of the time in her basket, rather. Time and again she came to the side of my bed to nuzzle me for reassurance, and every time I imagined that she wanted to spend a penny, pulled onmy dressing gown and took her down to the snow-covered front lawn, and she obligingly went through the motions of doing her duty.

She was sweetly patient for the two or three days she was confined to the spare room. I popped up to see her and give her a cuddle as often as possible. In the cold bleak February light at 5 o'clock in the afternoon, the time of Buffy's accident, I stood with her in my arms, looking out to the road, re-living the tragedy and grieving for her.

When at last Jock began to accept his new companion, I started to take them out for walks together, though I was desperately nervous at first, clinging tightly to their leads when a car came past and imagining danger when there was none.

Sheena came to us with the name Tiny on her inoculation

record, and we renamed her after her grandmother, after studying her pedigree certificate. She seemed rather wild and boisterous after Buffy, not having been schooled to the same degree of perfection, and she was highly excitable. She had a very strong maternal instinct, judging from the love she lavished on her dolly, and when she had been with us for a year we thought we would let her have a family. We heard of an eligible male, a handsome and well-bred Westie who would be glad to offer his services, and I invited him and his owner to tea.

With Jock safely out of the way for a couple of days, I prepared the bride, brushing her white silky hair until she looked a picture as she sat on the front window sill watching for the visitors.

When Ghillie arrived, it was love at first sight. Both were in raptures. We decided to dispense with all ceremony, and left them free to romp in the garden while their owners had tea indoors. The next afternoon, just to make sure, the process was repeated. The two went wild with joy.

We worked out the due date, and as the time approached we took her to the vet for a pre-natal check-up. But though the vet examined her carefully it was impossible to confirm whether she was actually in pup. She seemed more nervy than usual, but showed no other unusual signs.

I tried to prepare a nest for her in the washhouse near the back door, putting her basket in one corner, and plenty of newspaper all around. When the due day arrived she became very upset, and whimpered incessantly, refusing to settle down. This continued through the next day. We decided that it must be a false pregnancy like Buffy's, and did our best to calm her. How I wish, in retrospect, that we had called in the vet at that stage.

On the third day, when I came downstairs before

breakfast, before I had even opened the door that led from the hall, I heard a sound I could hardly believe. The unmistakeable little grunt of a new born puppy! Sheena was sitting up in her basket, intensely nervous as I approached. And there beside her was one tiny, perfect white puppy. I called Don down to witness the sight, and telephoned my mother and sister with the news.

But all was not well. The puppy was obviously weak, and Sheena was licking it desperately. Then I noticed that it was lying still and making no attempt to suck. I telephoned my mother again, frantic with worry, and she and Margie who had both had some experience of breeding Westies, volunteered to come over at once. The problem was how to examine the pup, with Sheena tense and possessive. I managed to entice her briefly into the garden, but she was back in a few seconds and when she discovered that her baby had been picked up she became quite frantic, and cried as if her heart would break, wailing at the top of her voice.

I took her upstairs with me and tried to restrain and comfort her while mother attempted to warm and revive the tiny puppy. But it was useless. By ten o'clock it was all over. Don buried the little body at the top of the garden. If only we had called the vet at the first sign of distress. The effort to struggle into this world had taken too long and had exhausted the pup. If only the birth could have been induced. If only I had realised the position and had sat up with her during the night . . .

Sheena was beside herself with grief all day, crying most sorrowfully and looking everywhere for her baby. She found a crust of white bread and picked it up tenderly, carried it to her basket and nursed it.

Next morning I was awoken at 5.30am by a high unearthly wail. In the half light of the late April dawn, with the birds beginning to wake, she was remembering the dawn of the previous day when her baby was newly arrived in her basket. I put on my dressing gown and went downstairs and sat with her on my lap for over an hour while she gazed down at the empty basket and cried inconsolably. Neither she nor I ever forgot the unbearable anguish. Poor little waif.

Six months later when she came into season her grief was renewed. Again one early morning I heard that eerie high-pitched wail, and when I went downstairs to comfort her I found that she had picked up a clean white handkerchief that had been left lying around and put it in her basket as if it were her baby. And like Rachael, she would not be comforted because it was not.

Every six months her grief was renewed again. For two or three days she would whimper continually and refuse her food, nursing her pink plastic squeaker with jealous love. I took her once more to see Ghillie. We found the house where he lived, and I rang the bell. No sooner was the door opened than the two dogs were in each other's arms. Again they were left free to romp ecstatically together in the garden for an hour or so.

But this time there was no pregnancy.

April 4th 1975 Jock's birthday – 14 years old. Took him right down to the lower meadow. He is rather overweight, but toddled along cheerfully after Sheena. At one stage when we had crossed to the far side of the meadow he lost sight of us and stood still, looking round in all directions (he is more than half blind and quite deaf.) So I said to Sheena: "Where's Jock? Go and fetch Jock!"

She raced over to him, passing close enough to brush against him, and he turned at once and started to walk back towards me – she is indeed his eyes and ears. The stream that runs alongside the meadow was very swollen after the morning's snow, and the current was quite strong. Sheena apparently didn't realise this, for she stepped down the bank expecting to paddle in the water as usual, but was immediately out of her depth. As the strong current began to carry her along she battled to swim to the bank. My heart was in my mouth as I yelled encouragement, but it only took her a couple of minutes to scramble ashore. She is a real water baby and loves to paddle, especially in hot weather.

For the past week she has been imagining she is pregnant again and has been highly nervous. Twice she has woken me in the mornings crying and scratching at the door. The first time it was 5 am and still dark. I had to go downstairs and sit with her on my lap to comfort her as I had done before.

July 6th 1975 Fourteen years tomorrow since we moved here, and fourteen years next week since Jock came into our lives. He is almost 100 per cent blind now, and noticeably more so in the last few weeks. He bumps into the furniture and can only just distinguish the light when the door is opened or the curtains are drawn, and he can apparently see Sheena when she moves across his line of vision. He is almost totally deaf; the only sound he seems to notice is a loud bark from Sheena. Apart from that he relies entirely on his senses of smell and touch. I have only to touch his coat lightly and he turns his head to try and see me. He is moulting and the hair on his face is thin and greyish now. He has lost his sturdy air of independence, and for the fist time since he was quite young I have been able to pick him up without angry snarls of protest.

Don's health had become worse and he was no longer able to do a full time job. He struggled valiantly with part-time work, doing the accounts for various concerns, but it had become necessary for me to take a full time job as librarian for an industrial firm, involving eighteen miles of devious cross-country driving each way. And company librarians do not merit company cars! After a great deal of heart searching debate we made the painful decision to put the cottage up for sale.

It was devastating. I had felt so sure that that happy garden and the great overlooking oak tree were going to be ours for life unless the way opened up for us to go back to Africa. The idea of uprooting ourselves for any lesser reason went hard against the grain; how could any other place ever mean quite so much to us as this, our first real home? But in the circumstances it seemed the only practical thing to do. The nearest shop was the tiny village stores over a mile away, and there were very few buses in to town, so that while I was away at work Don was, to all intents and purposes, stranded. And the car, my beautiful Triumph that had been the Car of the Year when I bought it, was already showing discomfiting signs of old age. And then, above all, there was the financial advantage to be considered.

We had a good offer for the cottage, and made plans for a half-way move to a small rented house nearer to my place of work where we could set up our base while we hunted for a permanent home.

But how would Jock cope with such an upheaval? How could we tear him away from his familiar territory in his present state of disablement?

The solution was taken out of our hands, mercifully. A few weeks before we were due to move we went out in the evening for a last game of bridge with some friends. When we came home there were spots of blood on the floor in the kitchen, apparently from Jock's mouth, though we could not confirm this as it would have been impossible to examine him without causing a major upset and risking a mauling in the process.

In the morning he lay in his basket, feebly licking traces of blood from his coat, and for the first time ever he refused to struggle out into the back yard as he had done every morning of his life. I stroked his thin body before setting out for work – for the last time, though I did not know it. Don phoned the vet later, and he called during the day and took him away in his basket, loading it in the back of his estate car. I rang him at six o'clock. He was a kind man and we had come to know him well.

"I'm afraid Jock is no more," he said. He had given him a light anaesthetic in order to examine him properly, but it was more than his weak system could take.

Jock was dead. R.I.P.

He was a game fellow, a dour little Scot with opinions of his own, but brimful of courage. His early morning rounds had dwindled to that tottering inspection of the border along the side of the yard, sniffing a little here and there before returning to the back door. He was a good trencherman to the last, always licking his dish clean and then inspecting Sheena's and polishing any scraps she might have left – she was by contrast a fussy eater.

So, sad though it was, the solution to our problem was miraculously timed, and at the end of November we packed and moved away with Sheena after fourteen happy years in the cottage. Twenty years, give or take, since that day of days when I had landed in Natal.

Next year came one of the greatest crises of our lives. It was an extraordinary summer. There was a long period of drought and the most excessively high temperatures in living memory.

I played a round of golf with a friend one weekend in

incredible conditions. The heat seemed to be reflected from the baked earth on the fairways, and we crept into the shade of a tree whenever possible during the round. Back at the clubhouse the temperature indoors was 93 deg F.

In Essex, not very far away, a temperature of 100 deg F was recorded one day; there were sixteen consecutive days with temperatures of over 80 deg and nine consecutive days when it reached 90 deg. We remembered Africa.

During those dog days Don's asthma flared up, in spite of the fact that the humidity was unusually low. In the early hours of Saturday July 17th, the whole countryside was blanketed with thick, stifling mist, triggering a bad attack, and before 7 am I called the night duty doctor. There was not much he could do, and he left with a warning that it might be necessary for Don to go into hospital.

Presently our doctor called, and he, too, thought that hospital would be the only answer. But Don, sitting propped up with four pillows in bed, refused to consider the idea. By noon though, he had to change his mind – he could hardly breathe. I rang the doctor, but he was still out on his rounds. I rang the chest hospital, begging them to send an ambulance; but this they could only do on doctor's orders. In near panic I rang the doctor's home again and left a desperate message. And in the very nick of time, when I thought the end had come, he arrived. A quick injection, and he picked up the phone to summon an ambulance. Minutes later the ambulance men walked into the front room where Don was sitting, unable to speak, with a light-hearted:

"Well, then, let's be having you ..." which faded into silence as they grasped the situation.

As the ambulance departed with Don inside, an oxygen mask over his face, I turned to the doctor who was standing by in his shirt sleeves:

"I hope he'll be all right."

"I hope so," he replied in a tone that made my heart sink even further.

Quickly I fed Sheena and shut her in the living room, got out the car and drove to the hospital with my mind in a turmoil. What should I do without him?

It took them two hours to bring him round. I was not a widow after all.

This shattering crisis was followed a month or two later by another, a complete nervous breakdown, and again Don was hospitalised. Again I thought I had lost him, this time to a world of unreality. It took long months for him to recover his co-ordination, and several years before he was truly his old cheerful self again.

In due course we left our rented home and moved into the little market town of Hadleigh. The house was nearly new, and suited Sheena well enough. There was a tiny garden at the back, and as it was in a cul-de-sac there was no passing traffic to worry about. Moreover it was near the local recreation ground, and a circuit round the tennis courts and putting green made a handy short walk. Further afield there were several good routes for dog walks of unlimited length.

Incredibly, we had been there less than a year before Don was struck down again. This time he was rushed by ambulance to the general hospital in great pain from a perforated abcess on the colon. Since he was taking steroids for his asthma, surgery was risky, and it was with fearful anxiety that I watched him wheeled away along the corridor to the theatre. But he survived not just the one, but two more operations to mend the damage.

Sheena

In 1978 we ventured forth on another Mediterranean holiday, flying this time to the island of Ibiza.We chose a tiny resort on the rugged and sparsely populated north coast.

Don was by no means fit. He was considerably overweight owing to the steroids he was compelled to take to control his asthma, and always short of breath in spite of the treatment. He was also suffering from general lethargy resulting from his breakdown.

When we arrived at the hotel we were disappointed to find that although it was close to the shore at the mouth of an idyllic little bay the path to the beach was too steep for Don to climb in his breathless condition. So he had to be content with a deckchair on the hotel terrace and a book, taking an occasional dip in the tiny swimming pool.

One afternoon I left him in his deckchair and went down to the beach to explore by myself. Unrolling my beach towel I ensconced myself for a while on the soft sand and sat there meditating and observing the other holiday-makers. Most were likewise deployed upon the beach, soaking up the sun in pairs or family groups, or bathing in the shallows. Two were lazily propelling themselves across the calm surface of the bay in a white pedallo; others were gathering near the rocks beside a glass-bottomed boat, preparing to set out on an observation trip.

From a little wooden shack set back from the main bathing area, lobster-skinned customers in floppy hats and sunglasses were carrying away cups of coffee and bottles of coke.

Looking around and absorbing the atmosphere, I experienced a strange sense of déja vu. I had the impression of a substantial ship moored in the bay, and of going ashore

56

with a throng of other people, the women in long dresses, visitors disembarking upon a foreign shore. Just as we were now, I reflected, though this time we had arrived by air.

Rolling up my towel and brushing the sand off my feet I put on my sandals and wandered across the beach to the farther side, where I followed a path through the pine trees and up towards the village.

In a shady spot just before the path joined the narrow tarred road I came upon what seemed to be a hippy trading stall, set out with cheap souvenirs – baskets, pottery and ornaments. In charge of the stall was a thin pleasant-faced woman, a vintage hippy person in a faded ankle length cotton skirt and steel-rimmed glasses. Encouraged by her friendly smile, I tried to talk to her.

"Do you speak English?" She shook her head. I knew barely half a dozen words of Spanish, so that was no good.

"Parlais vous Français?" I asked doubtfully.

At that she brightened up. I wasn't quite sure how to proceed.

I stroked the scraggy white poodle at her side. Then I noticed that the poor dog was crippled – it appeared as if all four of its legs had been broken at some time and had mended without being properly set. It must have suffered terribly.

"Oh, la pauvre petite!" I exclaimed, pointing to the misshapen legs.

Yes, she said, in half-understood French, reinforced by gestures, it had fallen off a table. I wondered how that could have happened, but it was beyond the scope of my French to elicit further details – and perhaps it was better not to know.

"Et moi aussi, j'ai une petite chien blanc," I said, wondering if there was a feminine form of the word.

We exchanged a few more pleasantries, groping for words. She said that she lived "with friends" along the coast – a hippy commune, I guessed. I told her that I was staying at the hotel, pointing across the bay, and that my husband could not walk far because of his asthma – demonstrating by clutching my chest and wheezing – and she expressed sympathy. I wandered on into the village.

As usual, I had taken more clothes than I needed for the holiday. On the last day of our stay I took out of my suitcase an unworn cotton shirt, folded it, and put it into a paper bag.

For the last time I picked my way across the soft, well-trampled sand past the bathers and sun-worshippers and up the narrow path on the other side of the bay. I handed the packet to my hippy friend, displaying the shirt.

"C'est pour vous, pour vendre – "

Perhaps she could add it to her wares. She was visibly touched, and thanked me with a seraphic smile. Perhaps that A level French had been worthwhile after all, I thought, as I made my way back to the hotel.

The highlight of our stay was the celebration of our twenty-first wedding anniversary – an amazing twenty-one good years of survival. I had a hair-do and put on my old wedding dress – it was a normal calf length and had had the sleeves removed – and we went to the hotel dance. Don managed gallantly to steer me round the floor a couple of times before he became too breathless.

JESSIE

Mother died just before Easter in 1979, and after that my sister Margie lived alone in the tiny cottage overlooking a nine-hole golf course. Alone, that is, except for the three Wigginses, three West Highland White terriers, stockily built Lesley and Topsy, and little Lavender.

Both Lesley and Lavender had earned their living by producing a litter apiece of pedigree pups. But Topsy, the youngest of the three, remained fancy free until Titus arrived on the scene that summer. He was a brindle lurcher type mongrel nearly twice her size, but he fell for Topsy hook, line and sinker. Margie made great efforts to keep them apart, but one May day when she was out he managed to break into the back yard of the cottage, and that was that. As Topsy's time drew near it was obvious that she was carrying an enormous litter, and when she reached full term she began to show signs of distress. She was examined by a vet and it was arranged that she should be taken to his surgery next day for an induction.

But Topsy couldn't wait. That night she gave birth to seven pups, the last one stillborn. Three of the survivors were white — or rather, cream – and the other three black. It was clear that she would not be able to nurse the whole litter, so Margie reluctantly decided to have the three black pups eliminated. An old countryman was called in to despatch them, while she averted her eyes.

In less than three weeks' time she was due to go up to Scotland, and she decided to take Lesley and Lavender with her in the car. Topsy and her family were left at home with their basket in the kitchen, the back door wedged slightly open so that she could get in and out, and the yard gate

59

firmly closed. A kind neighbour agreed to call twice daily and put food inside the gate for her. But Topsy would not let anyone outside the family into the house, so I drove over every evening after work to keep an eye on things, and was permitted to handle the pups. Which was just as well, because on one occasion I found one of them with its tiny head poked through a hole in the old blanket that lined their basket, and the consequences might well have been serious if it had not been extricated.

There were two males and one bitch, smaller than her brothers, and they were a playful trio. We would take them all out for a game in the lawn and watch as they wrestled boisterously, with fierce little growls. Then one by one they would give a big yawn and waddle back into the house for a nap.

When they were eight weeks old Margie began to look for homes for them. An advertisement in the local paper produced a shoal of enquiries. Sandy went first, then his brother.

Sheena had always longed for a family of her own. She cherished her rubber dolly, sleeping with it in her basket at night, and was miserable and highly emotional every time she came into season. After the tragic loss of her one and only puppy we had tried twice more to mate her. There was that joyous afternoon with Ghillie, her first love, but he was getting on in years, and nothing came of it. The next gentleman who was introduced was entirely different.He was not only inexperienced but distinctly unenthusiastic, so again there was no success. So it occurred to us to try and adopt a puppy for her, and Topsy's remaining daughter was offered for the role.

We consulted Sheena. She seemed quite taken with the idea of having "a little white doggy" to come and live with her, pricking up her ears and dancing with excitement. Perhaps she misunderstood, and thought we were proposing another boy friend.

Anyway, baby Jessica was brought to us on a warm Sunday in September. She had felt queasy in the car, and it was a subdued little bundle wrapped in a soft blue blanket that I gathered up in my arms and carried gently through the house into the back garden. We sat and talked to her while she unwound in the sunshine, and as she began to feel better she explored the grass around her. We kept an eye on her as we ate our Sunday lunch.

Sheena, meanwhile, did not seem overly interested, and because we could not be sure of her feelings towards the puppy we watched with some anxiety, hoping that she would not be jealous of all the attention focussed on the baby. That night I made a warm nest in a shallow wooden box, the kind that apples are packed in, and put it in the back room. There was a little wimpering at bedtime when I tucked Jessie up and left her, but she soon fell asleep, and Sheena came upstairs with me as usual and slept in my bedroom.

During the night, quite unusually for her, she decided that she must urgently go outside to spend a penny. Inevitably this meant disturbing the sleeping pup. As we went into the back room there was a gruff little bark from the sleepy Jessie, who raised her head but did not move from her nest. As soon as Sheena had performed her errand in the garden she returned, taking little notice of the puppy, who promptly went back to sleep, as good as gold. Sheena's curiosity satisfied, she too went back to her basket.

For the next few days we watched anxiously to see what kind of relationship would develop. Sheena seemed uncertain what to make of Jessie. She showed no hostility,but neither did she display any sign of maternal feelings. Instead, she adopted a boisterous attitude. She had always played rough games with her dolly, and when she started wrestling noisily with little Jessie I felt it was necessary to supervise very carefully in case she overstepped the mark and became too rough. When I was at work Don took over the task of supervision but he, too, became anxious at times. In fact we were both worried and constantly on edge from dawn to dusk, fearing that Sheena's high spirits might erupt into anger.

We dared not leave them alone together if we both had to go out at the same time. Jessie was too small and defenceless to be put at risk, and we simply could not gauge Sheena's real feelings. So Margie agreed to take Jessie back for a little while until she was bigger and better able to stand up for herself if need be.

Three weeks later we tried again. Gradually the two dogs seemed to settle down together. Jessie was a bundle of creamy velvet, her puppy coat deliciously soft to the touch. But I dared not cuddle her too much for fear of making Sheena jealous. If I stroked one, I had to caress the other with my other hand; if one of them jumped up on to my lap the other had to follow suit, and a glorious tangle of fur and legs ensued. More often Sheena would ensconce herself firmly in what she considered her rightful place on my lap while Jessie had to be satisfied with curling up under my chair, and I would reach down and stroke her surreptitiously. I would have loved to really cuddle her and give her the full attention that she deserved as my youngest baby, but Sheena's temperament was too volatile. After all, she had been my one and only faithful bodyguard for the past four years, since Jock died.

Gradually we all relaxed. Our fears subsided, and the

tension evaporated. I took them both out for short walks together, aristocrat and mongrel side by side. Sheena's coat was pure white – people often remarked that she must have been freshly shampooed; but in fact she was very seldom ever bathed. She seemed to keep naturally clean. Jessie's coat was very slightly creamy and shorter, and her ears were half drooped, whereas Sheena's were always pricked, true to her breed. Jessie grew to be two inches taller than Sheena. Her paws were enormous by comparison, her legs sturdier, and her tail was long in proportion to her body.

The winter passed uneventfully and spring came. We had some happy outings, one day, at Easter time, rambling on and on for a good two miles along an obscure footpath. On the way back poor Jessie kept stopping to sit down and rest her tired legs.

She still slept on her own on the canvas sun bed in the back room, where the south facing windows extend along the entire wall and look out on to the garden. At bedtime I would arrange her soft blue blanket, entice her on to the bed with some doggy chocs, and quickly, while she ate them, withdraw and shut the door, taking Sheena upstairs with me.

I enrolled Jessie for some obedience classes in the town. Though we only managed to get to a few sessions, she was very good and learned to "sit" and to walk alongside me and turn correctly, in spite of the hullaballoo caused by the motley collection of other less tractable novices.

As she reached her full strength and gained confidence, though, subtle changes were taking place beneath the surface. There were a few warning incidents, little flare-ups of temper and jealousy, promptly doused with a scolding, and, when peace had been restored, both were given extra petting. To be even handed was so essential.

All seemed to be well until one bright May morning. Sheena came downstairs with me and went towards the french window to be let out, while Jessie, as usual, came straight up to me, tail wagging, and jumped up to say good morning and have a hug. I greeted her and shoved her outside quickly behind Sheena.

Suddenly, without any warning, her pent-up jealousy erupted, and she flew at Sheena with a furious snarl, causing Sheena to yelp with pain and fright. I grabbed them both and pushed the terrified and bewildered Sheena back indoors, scolding Jessie. Shutting her out in the garden, I rushed to take Sheena through the sitting room and out of the front door to do her duty there. I was shaking with shock at the sudden outburst of rage.

That was the beginning of the end. From that moment the two dogs had to be kept in watertight compartments. Sheena was given the run of the upstairs rooms and hall and had to be let in and out of the front door to perform her duties. Jessie had the run of the back room and kitchen and took her airings in the little back garden. The sitting room was the no-man's land in between, and we had to be careful to see that one door was firmly shut before the other one was opened; the twain must never meet again. It was a dreadful nightmare.

I was still working full time and Don was perforce at home practically all the time for health reasons, restricted by his asthma, and also disinclined to do very much because of lingering depression. So that although I went home nearly every day in the lunch hour, he had to bear the brunt of the problem of the two separated dogs.

Sheena was and always had been completely devoted to me. She was my shadow all the time I was at home,

---

following me upstairs and downstairs and everywhere I went. She loved nothing more than to sit on my knee and be cuddled like a baby, leaning her head back against my chest, wanting to lick my face. I would not allow that, but let her kiss my neck and hands. I have never known a more demonstrably affectionate animal person. It seemed as if she could not get enough love, and she gave it unstintingly in return. I sometimes wonder whether as a puppy, brought down from Aberdeenshire to East Anglia, she had felt starved of love, and needed all the more to be reassured of it in adult life.

It is obvious with hindsight that the great mistake was to treat Jessie differently. I had tried to be even handed but failed. Perhaps if she had been allowed to sleep in the same room from the start things would have been better. I was glad that the carpet in the back room where she was confined at night was an old second hand one, diverted from a jumble sale, for it took heavy punishment as she gnawed away at the corners in the early mornings, giving vent to her frustration.

But it was clear we should have to part with her, sad though it was. I advertised in the local paper for a loving home for her. In the meantime, four days of highly nerve-racking watertight existence were as much as we could stand, and I took Sheena to some kennels "for a holiday", as I explained to her.

She had stayed there twice in the past. It didn't dawn on me for a long time afterwards how much she must have hated them, and how much it affected her attitude to being groomed, too. She had a long, thick and very fine coat which tended to get badly tangled, so that she sometimes looked very scruffy. When she was young I was able, with some difficulty, to keep her fairly tidy, though she never enjoyed being brushed and combed and was always impatient to get it over. As she got older she liked it even less, until eventually if I so much as tried to brush her she would bare her teeth, and even actually leave tooth marks on my hand – always showing the utmost contrition immediately afterwards, begging my forgiveness. It seems to be the natural instinct of the breed to resist 'interference' of any kind, but things were not improved by rough handling. Once when I went to fetch her home after a short stay at the kennels I was kept waiting some fifteen minutes before she was brought in. She had obviously just been freshly groomed, but her coat had been in such a tangled state when I took her there that it must have been forcibly done, and she was wild with excitement when she saw me. After that incident she was far more hostile when I produced her brush and comb.

But now I was thankful that she could go into sanctuary for what we hoped would be a very short stay. For the time being peace reigned at home, and at long last, if only for a brief spell, Jessie could have my full attention. She needed it, for she was a nervous wreck. I had heard of neurotic dogs, but now I understood what the term meant.

I was in a nervous state too, and I'm sure Jessie realised it. Having witnessed her outburst of temper I was half afraid that she might have a go at me, ridiculous though it may seem in retrospect. The problem was on my mind all day, even when I was at work. At home I talked calmly to her, trying to reassure her, but keeping a wary eye on her while I did the washing up, and she on me. But she was worried and puzzled rather than antagonistic.

Poor Jessie. It didn't dawn on me at first that all that was wrong was just intense jealousy and hunger for her fair share of openly expressed affection. It took days to heal the hurt. I took her out for short walks, but when we encountered another dog I begged its owner to keep it away from Jessie because she was in "a highly nervous state". She cringed at loud noises. The sound of clay pigeon shooting a couple of fields away quite upset her. This, though, was probably due to an incident that happened when she was a small puppy. Margie had been taking her home in the car when the windscreen shattered with a loud exposion, and Jessie had gone limp with shock – she thought she was dead, as Margie said afterwards.

However, by the end of the week both Jessie and I had recovered confidence, and she was a happy dog again, knowing that she was loved and without a rival on the scene. We had half a dozen replies to the advertisement and it didn't take long to find what sounded like a suitable home for her, though I was saved just in time from a near mistake. A family with young children wanted to have her, but it so happened that I had to drive past their house that weekend, and I discovered that they lived next to a busy by-pass. No place for an active young dog who could easily escape from the loosely fenced garden.

Instead, we agreed to let her go as companion to a very elderly widow who lived on her own in an isolated cottage deep in the Suffolk countryside, and had just lost her old dog. It sounded right for Jessie, peaceful and secure. It was arranged that I should drive her over to the widow's son's house in a village some twenty miles away, and he would inspect Jessie, and if all was satisfactory, would conduct me to his mother's cottage in Crowfield.

Though it was a relief to know that the drama was coming to an end I was very sad as I got the car out and laid down layers of old newspaper on the floor by the back seat, in case of travel sickness. As I settled Jessie in the seat I told her that she, too, was going away "for a holiday".

It was a beautiful day in late May, and under any other circumstances I would have enjoyed the drive. I found the terraced house where the son lived, and he came out to have a look at Jessie, who had been sick and was keen to get out of the car. She passed his inspection and it was decided that he should come with me to guide me to the old lady's cottage.

I pulled up as directed in a quiet lane with a tall hedge on one side, and slipping on her lead I let Jessie out of the car. All that could be seen of the cottage was a bit of ancient tiled roof almost completely hidden by the overgrown hedge. A grassy track led on into an orchard, but we went through a little gate on the left of the track, Jessie and I following our guide along a narrow garden path past clouds of lilac to the back entrance, a low stable-type door, the top half opening separately.

It is hard to describe the sensation that overwhelmed me as I stepped inside the house. It was like slipping back in time into one of the old cottage parlours glimpsed in my childhood.

I thought I saw old Mrs Norfolk, a scrawny figure in long dark skirts who had come to mother's help when my sister Ruth was born. The rag rug on the brick floor of her parlour, the shiny black-leaded range . . . It was almost eerie.

The little kitchen-cum-living room must have been unchanged for half a century or more. The one window was so small that at first the room seemed to be in semi-darkness. On the table was a budgie in a cage, beyond it an old-fashioned black coal range with a fire burning in the grate, though it was a warm evening. Beside the fire stood the old lady's upright armchair, and high above it a crowded mantelpiece.

Jessie

Jessie was introduced to Mrs.P., who smiled and patted her, and I sat down, a little bemused, on a plain wooden chair like the ones I remembered in the kitchen at home, long ago. The only incongruity in the room was the portable radio set on the table, which was playing cheerful music.

It was easy to realise how much a watchdog companion was needed in that remote situation. The nearest building was the village church which I was shown later. It was situated out of sight beyond the garden, hidden by trees and well away from the road, the only access being along a grassy path. The nearest houses were quite a long way off.

The old lady talked about her previous dog, and chatted on about better days when her greengrocer husband had cultivated the large garden now so overgrown, as well as the orchard, and had gone on his rounds in a horse drawn van to sell his produce. And she recalled an even earlier time before they came to Suffolk when the grower who had employed them both had supplied ornamental plants to bedeck the mighty steamship Titanic for her maiden voyage in 1912. Her husband had actually been photographed standing beside a potted palm tree on board the ill-fated liner just before she sailed from Southampton.

All this time Jessie was sitting quietly on my knee and I was inwardly dreading the moment of parting. At length I put her down, gave her a large bone to take care of and handed over her old blue blanket and her vaccination certificate. Then I made my farewells, and, telling Jessie very firmly to "stay", went out into the bright daylight, feeling like a traitor.

On my way home I was back in the past again, knowing exactly the desolation in the heart of a country mother in days gone by, as she retraced her steps along the quiet lanes after taking her child – one of many no doubt – to her first

----

"place" in service, leaving her to begin a strange and bewildering new life under an aged mistress. A kind-hearted mistress, no doubt, in a setting of idyllic beauty. But nevertheless I had handed my adopted child over to a stranger, and I had deserted her.

But Sheena was happy. She was brought home at once and restored to her rightful place as a member of the family. "We three", as we always called ourselves, were together again, to our and her immense relief. And yet I was heavy hearted for days, surprised to discover how deep the hurt went.

The trees were fresh with luminous green. Roadside verges were draped with the white lace of sheep's parsley, and may blossomed in the hedges. Blackbirds and thrushes shouted with triumphant joy late into the long light evenings, but the more exalted their song the more my heart ached for Jessie. I wondered how long it would take her to settle into her new role in her rustic environment, so sharply contrasted to the life she had known. She was used to seeing many people, meeting other dogs, and living in our light, wide-windowed modern house surrounded with all the noises of a small but busy market town. Surely she would enjoy the peacefulness; it must be a change for the better as far as she was concerned.

Twice that summer I felt compelled to drive over and visit her. The third time I made the journey, the following year, I found the cottage deserted. The old lady had died, I was told, and Jessie had been taken by a relative to live far away in the West country.

I still get a card from her every year at Christmas time.

SHEENA AGAIN

When I was made redundant again for the second time in my life I finally retired, from necessity rather than from choice. For a long time I continued to scan the situations vacant columns for at least a part time job. I had been looking forward for years to the time when my bread-winning days would be finished and I could spend more time on the golf course. But when the time came, I found my strength deteriorating due to misbehaving glands; after a couple of years I could no longer play eighteen holes, and reluctantly we both resigned from the club where we had made so many friends. It was too far away for social membership to be practical. This meant that "we three" were at home together a great deal more.

Sheena had always been one of the family, to be talked to and told everything – where we were going if we went out, who was coming to visit us.

"We're just going to the shops – we won't be long, Tiddles!"

Or "So and so are coming to play bridge tonight – you can sit with us and play too!"

Only occasionally was she banished to an upstairs room when we had visitors – if we had one of our very rare parties, or if the W.I. Committee came en bloc – and then she accepted the situation, always expecting to be allowed downstairs to meet the visitors before they left.

She slept in my bedroom. When she first came to us at Oak Tree Cottage she had the privilege of sharing our bedroom only for the first few days while Jock was adjusting to her

_____

presence in the house, and the loss of his dear Buffy. Thereafter, like Jock and Buffy before her, she was expected to sleep downstairs, and every evening the two wicker baskets were brought into the warm sitting room for them at bedtime.

After Jock died and we moved into our temporary home, Sheena's basket was still put in the sitting room for her, though she made it perfectly plain that she would vastly prefer to remain close to me all night as well as all day. And one day I relented – why not?

I folded an old lilac covered quilt and laid it on the trunk near my bed – my old fibre trunk that had accompanied me to South Africa and back. Sheena hopped up on it and sank comfortably into its depths, hardly daring to believe her luck. It was as if she were holding her breath.

She was a perfect picture, snowy white on the soft mauve background.

I had imagined that she might be restless, as she had been during those first nights when she was so unsettled, and I was half anticipating interrupted sleep. But not a bit of it. She was as quiet as a mouse, completely unobtrusive, as if jealously guarding her right to remain in that seventh heaven. There was no sound from her on that or any subsequent night – and when later I kept her basket in my room for her to sleep in the only sign of her presence in the dark watches of the night was the occasional creaking of the wicker-work as she changed her position, a very comfortable sound. It was only in her later years that she sometimes had bouts of snoring.

She did sometimes ask, even beg, to be allowed on to my bed, but that was strictly forbidden, except when she was not well. Periodically throughout her life she suffered from an upset stomach. It happened possibly every two or three months for no apparent reason. She would wake up one morning with her tummy rumbling and gurgling or, less often, she would start the day normally but would refuse to drink her breakfast milk, always an ominous sign, and the unhappy noises would follow soon afterwards and continue for most of the day. She learnt that when she was having one of these attacks then, and only then, she might jump up on to my bed to be comforted.

The reason for the attacks remained a mystery, unless her choice of food had something to do with it. When we first adopted her we were warned that she was a fussy eater, and that she certainly was. She had a small appetite and the only tinned meat that she would tolerate was a certain brand of cat food.

All this changed during the last year and a half of her life. I consulted the vet about the signs of stiffness in her legs, due to arthritis, and on his recommendation I gave her half a steroid pill every day. It had a magic effect on her appetite. It improved out of all recognition, and I started giving her a rather expensive type of dog meat which met with full approval. She began to put on weight, though she never became overweight, and we teased her about her "fat tum". It became much more of an effort to pick her up, and she could no longer spring up on my lap, with the extra weight and her stiff legs, but expected me to lift her up. Oh, my poor back!

I also consulted the vet about her strange bouts of shivering. Even on the warmest of days she would sit and shudder for no apparent reason. I was told that it was a nervous reaction in certain small breeds but he could give no explanation for it.

She was by nature a quiet and uncomplaining person. The only time she ever moaned or whimpered was when she was in season and feeling frustrated, longing for a mate. She was a lady of dignity and good manners, though she was excitable and my teasing sister could work her up into a frenzy of barking.

She was an old lady now. I dreaded the time when she might become incontinent, or need to be let out into the garden during the night, remembering Jock's later years, when the newspaper laid on the back door mat used to be sodden by the morning. But I need not have worried. Her habits were unvarying. When I got up in the morning she seldom stirred until the moment that I started to pull on my slacks. Then, for some unknown reason, she would immediately get out of her basket, come over to me for a close inspection, and then return to her basket or sit at the top of the stairs until I was ready to go down.

For some inexplicable reason she always showed signs of agitation when I made my bed, demanding my attention, and it was the same whenever I changed my shoes. Perhaps she associated these actions with the idea that one was about to go out and leave her on her own; we were told that when she was a puppy both her owners went out to work, one on day shift, one on night, and so it may be that the habit of watching for and dreading these signs of departure had become ingrained in her. Anyway it persisted for the whole of her life.

In the summer of 1985 we spent several weeks at Margie's house. The year after mother died she had left the tiny cottage overlooking the golf course and acquired a larger one with a big garden, and to it she added a corner of the adjoining field to form a paddock.

There was a strange assortment of animal life both within and without that fairly isolated cottage, ranging from the slimy to the sublime. From the revolting four-inch black slug which materialised above the wainscotting of the damp plaster wall in the dimly-lit sitting room one evening, causing me to run screaming to the furthest corner of the house, and followed shortly after it had been removed on a shovel by its equally revolting mate, to the four stately geese. They spent most of their time near their big bath of water in the garden, but made periodic excursions in single file into the paddock to graze.

It was pleasant to wake up on a summer morning to the sound of their quietly satisfied muttering as they passed beneath the window. They were very good watch dogs, creating a loud warning cacophony when strangers appeared, the gander advancing towards the intruder with wings spread, hissing fiercely.

And the oddest things happened. Waking early one sunny Sunday I sat up in bed and drew the curtains back carefully so as not to disturb the large spider in her nest at the top corner of one of them. Gazing across the paddock to its furthest point I saw a cock pheasant sunning himself on the grass, occasionally moving about and giving a throaty little "cock" call, master of all he surveyed. But what was the white object beside him? Could it be his mate, a freak albino pheasant, or was it a lump of chalk? At any rate it didn't move. I sat watching for perhaps a quarter of an hour, and then suddenly the mysterious object stirred – and a white cat moved gracefully away and disappeared into the adjoining field, leaving the pheasant on his own. The *owl* and the pussy cat?

The hand-reared lambs were a menace. They had reached the adolescent stage, restless and greedy in their orchard territory. One day a broody hen with her young family strayed through a gap in the fence into the lambs' corner of the garden. There was much loud clucking, and looking out

75

of the window I saw the lambs edging their way, heads down, nearer and nearer to the chicks. I leapt through the window to go to their rescue, but before I could reach them to my utter horror one of the lambs picked up a baby chick and ATE it. A carnivorous sheep! I could hardly believe my eyes!

But strangest of all was the saga of the Earwig. I like to take a glass of fruit juice to bed with me in case I wake up thirsty in the night. Usually I reach out and feel on the bedside table for the glass without turning on the light. The first time I did this in my sister's spare room I got a mouthful of something that was not pure fruit juice – in fact, it wriggled. As I switched on the light I spat out – an earwig.

The next night when I woke up feeling thirsty I was careful to put on the light before taking a sip – just in case. And sure enough, there was one of the little beasts swimming around in my drink.

On the third night I was determined to protect my fruit juice. I found a little plastic dish which just fitted over the top of the glass. That would fox them. I turned out the light, and quite a long time afterwards was just dropping off to sleep when there was a little clatter on the bedside table. And when I put on the light, there, enjoying his fruity swim, was a fat earwig, and beside the glass the plastic dish which he had pushed off the top of the glass.

The problem was finally solved by standing the glass in a protective moat – a saucer of water, though even then I always took the precaution of switching on the light and inspecting my drink before taking a sip.

Topsy, the last survivor of the three Wigginses, was Sheena's best friend and enjoyed having her to stay. We took Sheena's basket with us and as usual she slept near my bed. In the morning Topsy would scratch at the door and come in to say good morning to her guest. But Sheena was feeling her age now, and I had to help her up and down the steep twisting staircase and guide her from room to room with my voice.

Her birthday was on January 12th. I felt certain that the next one would be her thirteenth, but when I rummaged in my desk and found her pedigree certificate I was amazed and quite taken aback to find that she was in fact fourteen. It seemed scarcely a year since we had begun to think of her as an old dog, no longer in her maturity but an elderly lady. No longer able to jump up on to my lap, having first asked permission, but needing to be hoisted up bodily. Her slender little legs had become slightly bandy with arthritis, the strain on them increased by the fact that she had put on so much weight due to the PLT pills. Her sight was failing with the gradual appearance of cataracts, so that she would bump into furniture, relying more and more on the "feel" of the familiar premises to find her way about. Though she had surprisingly good tunnel vision and could spot people moving across her line of sight a good hundred yards away. Sometimes if I called to her she looked round the room trying to see me, and was quite at a loss until I moved, when she spotted me at once. She was a little deaf too, though she always heard my call, and responded even to normal speech.

The previous summer she had been stripped for the second time only in her life. In earlier years occasional light trimming had been sufficient to keep her tidy, but in old age her long, fine coat became terribly tangled and scruffy, and the older she grew the more she resisted my attempts to trim it. She was not only unkempt but uncomfortably hot in the summer, so she was taken to the vet for a light anaesthetic and professionally stripped.

Shorn of her long coat she looked so much smaller, and rather pathetic, and her bandy legs gave her a Charlie Chaplin appearance from behind. It was then that we noticed the small ominous lump on her tummy. Her coat started to grow again and soon she was looking sleek and trim without any effort on our part, and she was comfortably warm but not panting in the heat of the sun any more – though it was a miserable summer and there was little enough sunshine anyway.

But through the autumn months the lump gradually increased in size. Shortly after her fourteenth birthday I took her to the vet's surgery. As usual, she was absolutely petrified, and started to shake violently the minute she was carried over the threshold of the waiting room and realised where she was. When her badly overgrown toenails had been trimmed, I pointed out the lump. The vet felt it carefully, and then gave his verdict. A mammary tumour, with a 30 per cent chance of malignancy. Couldn't they operate, at once? No, I was told, at her age she wouldn't stand up well to surgery, and in any case the cancer had very likely spread and would be impossible to eradicate.

I sat down, weak at the knees. Eventually, he continued, it would ulcerate and she would have to be put down. There was nothing that could be done. It was very hard to accept.

"Just keep her comfortable, and give her half a dispirin if necessary."

It was hard to adjust to the agonising sense of doom, to realise that there was absolutely nothing that could be done to avert the inexorable course of the disease and arrest the multiplication of malignant cells in her little body. Nothing except pray for a miracle, which we did, over and over. I wondered how long it would be. Perhaps she would be with us until Easter. Perhaps she might last through the spring and into the summer. Please God let it shrink up and disappear altogether.

March 8th The tumour was now the size of a tennis ball, a burden she must carry with her until the end. We could not tell how she felt, but she seemed to experience inconvenience rather than pain. It made her restless, and sometimes she would get out of her basket and prowl around the bedroom and out into the corridor at night, not uttering a sound. In the daytime she did not lie and sleep for long in the same position, as she would normally, but turned often and tried to get comfortable.

With her "burden" adding to her already increased weight, and the joints of her small legs affected by arthritis, she had great difficulty in negotiating the staircase, though she refused to let it deter her. Where there was a will there was a way. If I went upstairs, up she would come too, and mostly I left her free to make up her own mind, arguing that the exercise was good for her and would help to keep her joints mobile.

It was a terrible winter, the coldest February for forty years. Every night the temperature dropped below freezing and sometimes remained there throughout the day as well, or rose two or three degrees at most above zero in the biting north easterly wind. There was ice on the road outside the north-facing front of the house, as well as a scattering of snow over the countryside, for the whole of the month and well into March.

What with the weather and the fact that in lifting Sheena I had acquired a slipped disc, a really crippling disability necessitating seven visits to an osteopath, Sheena had no outdoor exercise except for toddling round the small back garden on her own.

I lay on my bed for hours at a stretch, watching the leaden clouds pass slowly across the wintry sky, and Sheena lay on the floor nearby. She hoppity-hopped gamely upstairs after me each time I retired for the enforced periods of lying flat on my back, the only way to get relief from the pain. But the bedtime ascent last thing at night became a desperate problem.

After spending the evening snoozing on her chair in the sitting room, whither she climbed by means of two careful leaps - one on to the thick chair seat strategically placed on the floor for her, the next on to the actual chair – she would be sleepy and stiff. She had to be coaxed off the chair and persuaded to go out on to the lawn to do her duty. Provided it was not raining there was no great problem – she objected to getting her feet wet – and if there was snow on the ground she relished the outing and spent longer than usual in the freezing air.

The tricky part was the final ascent up the stairs when I went to bed. I was quite incapable of carrying her, and so was Don, with his weakened back. It was difficult enough to negotiate the stairs on my own, using a walking stick. But I could hardly bear to watch her pathetic attempts to follow.

She would mount the first step, wag her tail and stop to have a think. Then down, turn round and try again, puffing and panting, achieving perhaps three or four steps at the next attempt. Then another pause for rest, and down again. At last, perhaps ten minutes later, she would summon every ounce of strength, count one, two, three, go! And with a tremendous effort she would leap into her stride and gallop the whole way up, arriving very subdued and tired.

As the dark days went by and she got worse it did cross my mind that if this determined exertion should bring on a heart attack it might actually be the simplest way for her to go. Or better, though it was a painful thought, she might go in her sleep.

In winter I kept her basket in my clothes cupboard so that she was out of the draught, and there she slept, or tried to sleep, with the door propped open. One night I was woken by the sound of painting and gasping as she walked round the room in distress, and I found the door of the cupboard was shut. She must have come out for a nocturnal stroll and then pushed it shut by accident, so cutting herself off from her bed and her dolly.

March 12th. Sheena was sick several times during the night. Had she picked up an infection, or was it due to pressure of the tumour on her tummy? I was too incapacitated to do much, and Margie had to clear up the mess when she called the next day.

March 18th, Tuesday. The tumour was beginning to look inflamed and angry. Sunshine warmed the back room sufficiently to allow me to lie there on the low canvas bed after lunch, and Sheena managed to climb on too and lie at my feet in her very favourite position. So often we had rested in the sun like this in summertime. Towards three o'clock I remarked to Don that it was the time she would normally have had her walk, though she had refused to come out with me since last autumn. Yet now, unbelievably, she heard that remark and pricked up her ears. It was a bitterly cold day, but I put on my anorak and walked questioningly towards the front door. Yes, she would come out, she decided to my astonishment. I was even more surprised when, instead of just sniffing round the clumps of heather by the pavement, where brave sprays of purple and white were showing, she made it clear that she intended to set out on our accustomed route to the end of the square and round the corner.

Without going back to fetch her lead as I would normally have done – she felt more confident with the lead on after her sight deteriorated I said: "Alright then, let's go!"

And in spite of that monstrous tumour hanging beneath her tummy she tottered eagerly along, even going ahead of me, down to the corner and round towards the playing field. There she lingered on the turf for a few moments before I called her back – it was too cold to stand about. We walked very slowly homewards, while I called to her constantly to direct her. It was her first walk for four months, and her last.

March 19th. Wednesday. The tumour started to leak a little moisture, and she kept trying to lick it dry. The chill easterly wind still kept the temperature down. Hardly anything had started to grow; all the hedges were brown and dead and the only signs of spring were a few crocuses in bloom.

March 20th. Thursday. We stayed indoors all day except for a quick trip to the garage to get the car serviced. Sheena could not get comfortable. She lay in her armchair, having scrambled up in two stages via the thick cushion on the floor, settling first on one side, then on the other, constantly changing her position. She had gone out into the garden before breakfast and performed dutifully on the lawn, climbing back clumsily over the doorstep. She drank her milk as usual, but for the first time she refused to take the little piece of cheese in which her PLT tablet was disguised. Did she realise – was she accepting the fact that pills were no use to her any more? She ate nothing more at all except for a tiny crumb of cake.

By evening the tumour looked much worse. I watched the

last episode of Treasure Hunt on television, but all the time at the back of my mind I was wondering what we were going to do with her at bedtime. I could not carry her. and it was by now clear that with all the will in the world she would never manage to climb the stairs again. Ought I to summon the vet there and then to end it all?

Don always retired about seven; so I was surprised when he appeared in his pyjamas as if summoned by telepathy. If I fetched her basket, he suggested, we could between us get her into it and carry her upstairs.

Somehow, holding the basket on the cushion in front of her chair, we managed to slide her gently into it, and then slowly and laboriously we carried it between us up the stairs and pushed it inside the cupboard into its usual position.

Sheena hardly moved. She lay so still and dazed that I thought again how merciful it would be if she were to pass away in her sleep. I put her squeaker into the basket beside her and she acknowledged it with a slight movement of her head. Sleeping or waking, she kept perfectly still all night, and I had to look very closely to see if she was still breathing when I got up.

I dressed and got ready to go downstairs,and she struggled out of her basket. Another impasse. It was solved by putting a soft scarf under her chest like a girth, clipping her lead on to her collar, and half lifting her sideways down the stairs, one step at a time. Still half carrying her I got her through the living room, out of the french window at the back and on to the frost covered lawn where she performed as dutifully as ever, and then made her own way slowly indoors again.

This time she refused both her milk and her pill. Nor could she get up into her chair via the cushioned step. I folded an old cream candlewick bedspread and put it down for her on the hearthrug. And as she lay there I saw the first signs of blood. The tumour was in an appalling state. She made a feeble attempt to lick it but soon gave up.

The time had come at last, the time I had been dreading. It was 8.45 when I rang the vets' surgery and asked to speak personally to the one vet (out of a team of four) who knew Sheena. I told him she had come to the end of the road, and that since neither Don nor I could lift her we could not bring her to the surgery. Nor did we want to take her there, to the place that terrified her so much. He grasped the situation and promised to call in the afternoon.

From then on I spent every available minute with her. Several times she accepted a drink of water. And all through her last hours, though half dazed with weakness, she kept turning her head slightly to make sure that I was with her. I prayed the end might come soon – perhaps even before the vet arrived.

To be with any animal at the moment of departure is moving. It was so with the sick old ewe lying in the field next to the Old Vicarage earlier. I had had nothing to do with her, but I happened to be crouching beside her when she breathed her last; and I felt suddenly bereft.

It was so with the little black velvet mole that Jock dispatched. He was always fascinated by moles and molehills, of which we had plenty in the garden at Oak Tree Cottage, and you only had to point to a freshly dug mound and say: "Look, there's a pouffer!" and he would leap upon it and start digging furiously. This particular mole had been burrowing below ground near the stream in the water meadow when we were out for a walk, Jock and I. Jock attacked the mound with great vigour and pounced upon the occupant. A quick nip in the neck and he was suddenly motionless, half out of his burrow, his big yellow paws spread out, his little snout pointing heavenward. I grieved for him.

It was so, a thousand times more so, now.

To begin with, we ourselves had to make the decision, to gauge when the right and inevitable moment had come, when the deed could no longer be postponed. We wanted her with us as long as she herself wanted to stay. At fourteen, even in the best of circumstances, we could not expect to have her with us for more than another twelve months at the most. But in spite of her stiff legs, dim sight and partial deafness she could have survived happily for quite a while but for the tumour.

She had until the last few days been lively and in good spirits, dancing attendance on us when I brought in the teacups at "biccy time", pricking her ears with interest when I pointed out her friend the pussy cat in the garden, and looking altogether better than Jock had done when he died at fourteen and a half years old. If only it hadn't been for that monstrous tumour.

As the weeks went by we had watched it grow daily larger and more menacing, the dreaded day drawing inexorably nearer. And now it had come, just nine days before Easter. It was Bad Friday. Now, I thought, even Sheena herself would want to go.

I watched her closely. She lay so quietly that it was impossible to know whether she was in pain, but she must have been suffering greatly. Once she stretched her head forward and arched her back and I was afraid she was going to struggle. I touched her gently and promised her over and over that everything was going to be all right, and that the "doctor man", as she knew the vet, was going to come and help her. With a dreadful sense of finality I undid her collar and slipped it off. She was shuddering intermittently, as she had been in the habit of doing for over a year for some inexplicable reason.

At four o'clock the vet arrived to administer the last rites.

She struggled to her feet when he approached her, but hadn't the strength to resist as he examined her very briefly. He lifted her gently on to her armchair and prepared the syringe. Don warned him that she was liable to bite, so he slipped a gauze gag over her mouth, though it seemed hardly necessary. I was instructed to hold her head. There was no resistance. Holding up her foreleg he deftly snipped the hair to enable him to locate the vein. Nobody spoke. As the needle was withdrawn I asked, "Can I let go?"

And she flopped limply over on to her side and laid down her burden for ever.

The gag was slipped off. The white ears were still pricked, mouth and eyes closed, and she lay still.

Her spirit, her very presence remained with us for days and perhaps weeks. We mourned for her, but knew that she was happy now. Perhaps romping with her beloved Ghillie, father of her puppy, perhaps with her little white baby. Or, who knows, perhaps she has started another lifespan in a warm soft litter of pups. She is still alive somewhere, of that I am certain.

For the first time in twenty-five years Don and I were dogless. We were both heavy-hearted and I wept for her. On the fourth day I wrote an account of her passing and found that the act of setting down my feelings in words had lightened some of the heavy grief.

But how we missed her. I missed the creaking of her wicker basket as she moved in the night. I missed the daily rituals, the unlocking of the french window to let her out first thing in the morning, the tea-time biccy routine, the nudging and tail-wagging reminders that din-din time was drawing near.

It seemed dreadful to throw away the scraps from our supper plates, gravy or fish skin or other tit-bits that she loved. And the final outing to the garden at bedtime followed by the hoppity-hop up the stairs to bed, the constant presence of my little minder.

She gave so much love. Always, even in her old age, she wanted a "kiss and a cuddle" at least once a day – she kissed me and I cuddled her. In her more active years she would come up to my chair wagging her tail and requesting permission to jump up on to my lap for the purpose. When she grew too stiff to jump up, she would present her request and then turn half sideways into position so that I could reach down and haul her up. My neck had to be well and truly licked, and then she would turn and settle herself comfortably on my lap, facing forwards. Unfortunately during her last month I was unable to lift her because of my slipped disc, and she had to make do with an apology and plenty of stroking.

She loved to lie stretched out in the sun in the back room, or, even better, to lie beside me on the canvas sun bed when the days were warm enough. Or she would sit, long suffering, in my study upstairs while I wrote – but only for so long before her patience ran out. Then she would go and fetch her squeaker, forcing her attention on me until I broke off from whatever I was doing and had a game with her.

She loved her Daddy too and had been company for him in the long hours when I was out at work or otherwise engaged. We had survived so may crises together, and she herself had known such tragedy. The memory of her distress when she lost her only puppy still makes my heart ache. We three had been long together and understood one another, and our lives were closely intertwined. Bereft indeed were we without her.

Her sturdy, independent friend did not survive her for many months. Shortly after Sheena's death Margie noticed an ominous swelling on Topsy's tummy. It grew rapidly larger, just as Sheena's had done. She was taken to a vet, and this one took a different view to that of Sheena's "doctor man". She offered to operate at once and remove the tumour, and Margie thought it was a chance worth taking. Topsy was a tough customer and apart from getting heavier and slower showed little sign of senility, though she was about the same age as Sheena. She had recovered well from a hysterectomy the previous year.

The tumour was removed and all seemed to go well but the vet's report was not good. The malignancy had spread beyond the actual tumour.

In less than three months she became uneasy, constantly licking the sore red patch on her tummy. She lost her usual vitality and her strength declined.

To the very end her favourite place was the back of Margie's old estate car where she spent long hours, whether it was parked at the stables where Margie worked or in the garden at home, or rattling around the countryside. So when the vet came to put her to sleep it was there, in her familiar resting place, that she breathed her last and went to join Sheena and Lesley and Lavender in the happy hunting ground.

BLACK-EYED SUSIE

August 10th 1986. Sunday Yesterday Margie drove me to a village beyond Lakenheath to see a twelve-week old Cairn puppy. The long drive home, with said puppy on board, was one of the most exhausting and traumatic experiences I have known.

I should have had the sense to take a large cardboard box and put her in it, instead of imagining that I could hold her on my lap. I had remembered fetching Buffy when we brought her home to Oak Tree Cottage for the first time, and how I had held her on my knee. She had been nervous but amenable, but then she was a year old and well trained. This one was very small, unused to wearing a collar and lead and as slippery as an eel, trying all the time to claw her way up on to my shoulder or down on the floor of the car. Harvey, Margie's newly acquired merle collie, was in the back and persisted in poking his long nose over my shoulder to sniff at the strange and lively scrap.

It was a hot day and the journey seemed endless. At least, as Margie remarked, she must be healthy to struggle so hard and so persistently. She is like a miniature Alsatian, with dark pointed ears and brindle coat, her eyes like shiny black buttons. "Black-Eyed Susie" – or shall we call her Pixie? (Her mother's name is Dixie.) Actually it is not her eyes that are black but the markings round them, and her whole face is more black than brindle.

She slept in the sitting room. We are thankful that her owners had started to train her to sleep on her own away from her mother and her West Highland "aunt". There were

----

frustrated squeals towards six a.m., so I took her outside, and when she came in her paws were wet with dew.

She plays boisterously, just exactly as Sheena used to, with Sheena's old rubber dolly – or rather its head, which amazingly still has some hair on it, and with bits of cauliflower stem and other rubbish from the compost heap under the bushes. Ten minutes' rest after breakfast, then fresh explorations. She mastered the art of climbing upstairs easily, but cautiously – like Buffy she had never known stairs before.

August 14th. Susie has her meals at noon, and five o'clock, and then last thing at night to make her sleepy and ready for bed. On Wednesday, her fourth day with us, for the first time there was silence when I had settled her down and shut the door for the night. Incredible relief. But she still wakes us at about six, scratching on the door and sometimes resorting to deep, resentful baying if her summons is not obeyed.

She is not going to be just my shadow, as Sheena was. She makes it very plain that she loves her Daddy, and her Daddy spoils her dreadfully, allowing her on his bed and holding long conversations with her in baby language. "She is a joy," is his verdict.

I still think about Sheena and miss her a lot. I see her stretched out on the carpet in front of me now as I sit in the "sun room", turning her head every now and then to make sure that I'm there. I even talk to her. I wonder if she hears?

Susie busies herself unceasingly. She unravels the corner of the carpet when I am not looking, chews the wicker dog basket, brings in ancient bones long buried in the garden. She chases her tail, turning cartwheels with it held in her mouth. She pulls up mouthfuls of grass from the lawn and excavates the roots, and has to be chastised for nipping at

----

one's socks or cuffs.

She is a very independent little girl, playing by herself on the lawn with her assorted toys. At the moment she has Dolly and Squeaker as well as her own soft toy with its fascinating built-in rattle, and she is prancing in circles with it in her mouth in the bright sunshine. She is not as keen to be cuddled as Sheena was, not yet, anyway, but is restless when sitting on my knee. Such purgatory on that traumatic car journey.

Incredibly, at only twelve weeks old she has shown signs of being in season. Impossible, they say; yet overnight little discolourations appeared on the newspaper put on the floor to protect the carpet, and a number of times she has gripped my arms with her forelegs and arched her small back with urgency. Little nymphomaniac.

August 31st. Susie has just learned to jump up onto chairs, and this morning for the first time, tired out after a breakfast-time romp with Dolly, has curled up for a nap in the big armchair in which Sheena breathed her last. I had explained to her that it was Sheena's Dolly, "but Sheena would let you play with her – Sheena's a good girl."

She is growing very fast. The longer hair of her adult coat is beginning to appear, especially on her neck and in tiny ripples along her back. Her eyes are still like shiny black almonds, though on closer inspection they are seen to be brown, especially obvious when she rolls them coyly. Her coat is getting slightly lighter in colour, more of the silvery wheaten shade, though there are predominantly black markings on her ears and muzzle and bands of greyish-black and brown flecks elsewhere.

September 7th. I'm sure she is bigger than Jock was at this stage. Her weight must have doubled in the four weeks we have had her. She is eating ravenously, still having milk for breakfast and three good meals through the day. Her energy is amazing. Sometimes she "goes mad" as Jock used to do, bolting round and round the garden and into the house, round the downstairs rooms and out again like streaked lightning, her tail tucked between her legs like a greyhound at full tilt. When she chases her tail she turns into a cylindrical dynamo, spinning round so fast and for so long that I worry that it must affect her in some way – how can she not get dizzy?

I wish her needle-sharp milk teeth would hurry up and come out – one's hands get quite sore from being playfully chewed, though there must be another two months to go before her grown up ones appear. She can "mouth" one's fingers gently and caressingly without hurting them, but the moment she gets excited and forgets herself she can deliver a really playful nip.

The back garden is very small, but for her it is a vast adventure playground. She has excavated huge caverns by the further fence where she can burrow away out of sight to her heart's content behinds the geraniums and montbretia.

Luckily she can do little damage there, in fact she is helping me by digging up masses of the thick white creeping roots of bindweed, and it keeps her happily occupied. At other times, when there has been a long ominous silence I look out to see what mischief she is up to, only to see her lying on her back playing with a small stick or an old bone, juggling it between her paws and chewing it lazily from time to time.

Sometimes there is a sudden outburst of high-pitched yapping, a blend of anger and fright – she has spotted a hostile object lurking in a corner by the ivy covered wall. It usually turns out to be a leaf flapping in the wind (it happens mostly at dusk or after dark.)

The loudest barking and greatest excitement is aroused by the sight of a pussy cat on the roof, generally the black and white one that was Sheena's special friend, though there are several others in the vicinity. Sheena used to make friendly advances to it and allow it to have its daily nap under the cupressus tree. This was a very happy state of affairs unless Topsy paid us a visit, for she was an inveterate cat chaser, and at the first sight of her, pussy had to beat a very hasty retreat.

I believe that Susie would like to make friends with it – she had known a cat at her previous home – but her approach is much too boisterous at present. Up on the roof the cat knows it is safe, and Susie is wildly frustrated to see it so tantalisingly out of reach. It is a pity she has no dog or cat companions that she can befriend.

But she is a very happy person, very much an extrovert. One can almost hear her chuckles when she plays by herself, and she definitely smiles when her tummy is tickled. She is indeed a joy.

Her favourite plaything at present is an "apple ball". It will roll at the slightest touch of a paw and can be thrown and retrieved endlessly – or until the thrower is worn out. One game she enjoys is to carefully manoeuvre the apple underneath the bureau in the sitting room and then, when it is hidden from view and out of her reach, she will come and tell me she wants her apple.

So I am obliged to get a walking stick and wiggle it about under the desk until it pops out. Then the whole ploy is repeated. Sheena used to play the same game, though not with such maddening persistence. The only answer is to push some thick telephone directories under the bureau to block the access.

_____

Sitting in the garden in the September sunshine I ponder on the difference between the Cairn and West Highland temperaments – or is it just an individual contrast between Sheena and the others? She always seemed to need me. I remember that first night, how often she came to my bedside to assure herself that I was there, in her strange new surroundings. And how even on her dying day she turned her head frequently to look for me. If she were with me in the garden now (and who knows, perhaps she is,) she would be lying, panting, no doubt, beside my chair. If I went indoors she would follow at once.

Whereas Susie, admittedly brimming with youthful energy, will not stay close even if I call her to do so, but is constantly on the go, running up and down chasing butterflies and bluebottles or inspecting the lawn inch by inch for some purpose best known to herself, totally ignoring my presence. If I go indoors she continues to play happily as long as the french window is left open. If I close it from inside she immediately comes out and paws at the glass, requesting me to open it again – her line of retreat must always be open.

She is a great acrobat, leaping at the shrubs, tearing off the leaves and hanging on to overhead branches with all her might, tugging and jumping up and down until they are torn off. She would defoliate the Elaeagnus completely if she could. It needs pruning anyway.

September 23rd. A hot, Indian summer day. I found Susie in the kitchen playing with the water in her drinking bowl, scooping it out with her big front paws and making a swampy mess on the lino. I put some cold water in a big plastic washing up bowl and set it out on the lawn for her. At first she chose to ignore it, running about and leaping up at the Elaeagnus. But when I came indoors and left her alone, curiosity overcame her, and soon she was immersing first her nose and then both front paws at once in the water, then biting the rim of the bowl and uttering squeals of frustration because she couldn't tip it over. She is going to be a water baby like Sheena and Jock before her - they both liked to paddle whenever possible.

Last week we had an Intruder. One night when I let Susie out at bedtime she set up a loud frantic yapping, much more urgent and excited than usual. Oh dear. This had happened before. I remembered the horrified excitement of Sheena one evening at this time of year, and, much earlier, the same reaction from Jock at Oak Tree Cottage. I found a torch; my worst fears were confirmed. There in the shadows, quite close to the house, was the rounded form of a hedgehog "in full bristle". With some difficulty I grabbed Susie and got her indoors so that the poor animal could get away, and, incidentally, to give the neighbours some peace and quiet! Somehow he must have come from the garden of the old peoples' home which backs on to our garden. Armed with the torch I went out and removed the small section of wire netting that blocked the one vulnerable corner, so that the hedgehog could return whence he must have come. (Or so I thought.)

Next morning I replaced the wire very carefully, making sure it was virtually impossible for the wiliest of hedgehogs to get through.

But either he had miraculously remained concealed in our garden, or else he had another extremely well camouflaged entrance, for when I let Susie out at bedtime the next night, the excited barking began again, and there, only a couple of feet from the french window, was the brave little ball of tawny spines. I shut Susie upstairs with Don, and summoning all my courage I knocked on the neighbours' front door. I felt rather foolish.

"There is a hedgehog in our garden . . .!"

But I was concerned for the safety of the hedgehog, and at a loss to know what to do. Help was forthcoming, and the intruder was scooped gently into a large cardboard box, carried away and set free some distance from the house. Now we can breathe more easily. The garden should surely be easily made hedgehog-proof, bounded as it is by chain-link fencing on the far side, a ten-foot high brick wall on the west and a woven-wood fence on our neighbour's side. Or could that fence be climbed?

Since it was suggested that Horace might have been looking for drinking water, I removed the old earthenware dish that had lain outside on the paving stones, in case it had been an encouragement to him. I learned incidentally that the staff at the old peoples' home regularly feed hedgehogs at the back of the home, so it was not surprising that he should wander so close to our house.

September 25th The impossible happened – Horace appeared outside the door again last night. I got Susie indoors and waited over an hour with the light on to encourage him to go away. When I let her out the coast was clear.

The mystery of his comings and goings was solved by Susie herself. When out neighbour reported that a small black Cairn nose was busily poking through a hole at the base of the wooden dividing fence I went to investigate. A small section of wood had been broken off leaving a gap of no more than two or three inches high beneath the fence, shielded from view by ivy. Just large enough, apparently, for a determined hedgehog to squeeze through. It was easily blocked.

October 19th Susie has discovered that with careful calculation and maximum thrust of her strong hind legs she can jump right up on to my lap. It is an exciting achievement for her; and for me a real thrill as she lands solidly on my knees to be cuddled and then sits quietly while I talk to her or read. It is a sign that I am accepted.

She has grown quite heavy – almost her full weight I should think. Her coat is beautifully thick and shiny and is growing longer, noticeably round her neck, and there is a soft black fringe round her ears.

October 25th What is not developing very markedly is her notion of obedience. In that way she resembles Jock, who was always inclined to be independent, to put it mildly. Susie tends to be deaf to our calls to come indoors from the garden. She is very much an outdoor type, a little gypsy who would be perfectly content to live in the open air, even after dark. She will play happily in the garden for hours, sometimes coming to the french window and, standing up on her hind legs, beating n the glass with her paws demanding attention. Sheena used to give a little scratch on the woodwork when she was ready to come in and then sit there patiently until I opened it, only repeating the signal if I was very slow in coming.

But when I open it for Susie, nine times out of ten she will immediately rush away and resume her play, having made sure that the house was not deserted – "Only wanted you to open it, stupid" she seems to say.

I am trying by dint of giving small rewards to train her to come promptly when called, but it is a weary business, and annoying too, when it is freezing and one wants to get her in quickly and shut the door.

I try as far as I can to give her a short walk on the lead every day. She is very slowly getting used to being restrained and guided, but it goes against the grain for her – she tugs at the lead and tries to pull me along full tilt, and would choke herself breathless if I did not forcibly check her and make her stop from time to time.

The world outside is so huge and exciting, dry leaves need chasing, even parked cars and babies in push chairs are intriguing – but why doesn't *everybody* stop to talk to me when I pant and strain at the lead to talk to them?

Pussy cats raise the blood pressure and have to be avoided at all costs, and thank goodness we have not yet had a close encounter with a hostile dog. I have not attempted to train her to walk to heel yet; it will have to come gradually, if at all. Obedience is only one of the aims of our walks; another is to familiarise her with her surroundings and enable her to get her bearings, just in case she ever finds herself loose,which heaven forbid. The next hurdle will be to take her out of our cul-de-sac, away from the recreation area and into the street. Sheena hated busy traffic and flatly refused to go into the High Street in her old age.

Susie's greatest toy now is her ball, an old green tennis ball presented gratis buy the sports shop. It is perfect. Until now she has played with apples. They will roll, but not very far, and soon get brown and uninteresting and have to be discarded. But the "ballie" bounces beautifully and runs forever. She is getting quite skillful at catching it when it is bounced towards her. But she tries her tiresome game of pushing it out of sight under the bureau unless the space is blocked up.

Another ploy is to take it up to the top of the stairs, put it down, and very gently nudge it – and over it goes, bumping to the bottom of the stairs while she follows, intrigued.

November 7th Surely she won't grow any bigger? She is a heavy weight on my lap, and her narrow collar is let out as far as it will go as her neck thickens and her lovely strong coat grows longer. When suddenly I come upon her soundly asleep on her back in an armchair, her body slightly curved, legs in the air with paws folded over, all velvety fawn and gold and charcoal streaked with black, she is beautiful beyond belief.

November 15th The days are getting very short. Susie spends as much time as ever in the garden, even when it is dark, and sometimes it isn't easy to discover what she is up to. Digging a new hole, perhaps, or listening to the secret sounds in the undergrowth, or just communing with the dark world.

Sheena used to do that when she was let out at bedtime. She would move a few paces away from the house and just stand motionless for perhaps five minutes, turning her head slightly from side to side, her radar switched on. I wonder what messages came to her. Was she in tune with infinity, saying her evening prayers?

Susie blends in with the shadows and it is very difficult to distinguish her as she flits about in the semi-darkness. When she realises that she is being watched she darts away to hide behind the hydrangeas, slipping from shadow to shadow. Eventually she emerges when the game is up and leaps about on the lawn, pouncing with both feet together on imaginary prey. Little imp of darkness.

A question has been on our minds from the beginning: will she be happy with us? Will she accept what we have to offer and be content to lead a quiet life with two rather inactive people, and only such a small garden? Is it not presumptuous to expect it?

There is now no doubt about the answer. It is expressed in the way she plonks herself down on our feet and curls up in contented possession. We are privileged to be thus taken over.

She talks to us. "Yowl . . ." means she wants to go out, or to do something different; it is often followed by a yawn, long tongue curling. Plaintive whimpers when she can't find a suitable hiding place for a biscuit or a bone, or wants her ball extricated from underneath the bureau. Or worried growls when she attempts to balance the unwieldy length of the old hazel walking stick in her mouth, or scolds and shakes her dolly like a dead rat. Sometimes when I have to mop up a"mistake" she has made on the carpet I scold her, and she in turn scolds dolly, passing on the blame.

Her new teeth have come – suddenly the sharp baby spikes have been replaced by smoother glistening white ones that don't puncture the back of one's hand so easily. Rolling over on to her back, she takes hold of my fingers in a gentle love bite, pretending to sink her fangs into the flesh, but barely holding on.

November 28th Susie is six months old now and any day she may come into season for the first time. She certainly seems more excitable, sometimes begging to be let out of the front door, which is not allowed except on a lead. She is taking more interest in the outside world and has a new lookout post, an upright chair from which she can just see out of the front window and watch out for cats. To get a better view she sits up in a begging position, waving her front paws to maintain her balance, ears pricked, watching intently. Walked her right round the tennis courts for the first time – one of Sheena's regular short walks.

December 2nd No more long undisturbed evenings. She'll rest while we have our supper and for a little while afterwards before she demands the freedom of the garden – whatever the weather. If it is raining she will play under the bushes, though she doesn't at all mind getting wet, unlike Sheena who had to be pushed out of doors if there was a risk of getting her feet wet. When eventually I entice her indoors again she expects a ballie game or a bout of wrestling. If neglected, she sits quietly in her armchair chewing the old candlewick cover, swallowing mouthfuls of it. After her late supper at about half past eight it's out to play again. By 9.30 she is getting sleepy, and from then until Don goes downstairs in his dressing gown at 6.15 next morning, there is peace.

She always sleeps in the sitting room. Until recently I shut the door when I came up to bed, leaving her curled up on one of the chairs. When we felt that the time had come when she could sleep with me as Sheena had done, I left the door open, anticipating great satisfaction when she found that she was welcome to come up with me. But she did not stir, and now she always stays downstairs on her own by choice, with the door open.

December 14th When we were out yesterday Susie broke open my plastic pill bottle and ate four cortisone and one anti-thyroid tablet, as well as chewing up a biro.

The daily walk is a formidable challenge, especially since the day she slipped her collar. She tries every time to repeat the process. She pulls me along, nearly choking herself, only pausing if she detects interesting dog or cat smells by the way. Today she spotted a black cat as soon as we were out of the door and her yowls were enough to waken all the inhabitants of Meadows Way from their Sunday siestas. We always go out soon after lunch as there are fewer dog-walkers about at that time.

She has made a fresh crater in the border against the garden wall, no doubt finishing off the hyacinth bulbs in the process. She has pruned off all the lower branches of the Eleagnus very efficiently and stripped as much ivy and honeysuckle as she can reach from the wooden fence on the other side. And still she hangs on to any boughs she can reach, tugging with all her might and jumping up and down.

These antics are accompanied by such desperate moans one would think she was in pain. I'm sure the neighbours think we torture our dog. I suppose there must be a therapeutic element in the exercise and that it enables her to work off some hidden frustration.

January 11th 1987 Susie's first experience of snow. In the late afternoon yesterday she sat gazing out of the window at the slight, tentative fall of small flakes. It was freezing at the time so that by nightfall there was a thin powdering of snow on the ground.

This morning it lies an inch or two thick and the fascination of the garden has increased tenfold. She would like to stay outside all the time, prancing around and tossing a small snow-covered fir cone in the air, and exploring everywhere with her nose buried in the snow so that she carries a little white rosette on the tip when she looks up. Happy as a sand boy – or rather, a snow girl.

After a while I persuade her to come indoors into the warm. She licks the snow from her paws and has a rest, but before long she is imploring me to let her out again.

We have been worried about her habit of chasing her tail and trying to bite it, apparently in some distress, mostly in the evenings. She was wormed before Christmas, which should have eliminated the most likely cause, but the twirling habit still persists. The vet has checked her anal glands and found nothing wrong, and he frightened us by telling us of a Jack Russell terrier so obsessed with its tail that it had to be put down. So we scold her now when it happens and try to divert her attention to some other game.

The visit to the vet was quite traumatic. Don came with me to hold her in the car and we both took her into the waiting room, but it was a struggle to hold her still. She is like a tightly sprung coil, full of amazing energy and very strong for her size. It will take a great deal of patience and a lot of car journeys to train her. The daily walk is still something of a trial as far as I am concerned.

January 13th The snow is now nearly six inches deep. No more walks while the freeze-up continues. But Susie has a hilarious time in the garden, which started when she discovered that tugging on a branch, her usual game, caused an avalanche of snow to cascade down all around her.

We still have occasional qualms, wondering at our temerity in adopting her and expecting such a fiery ball of energy to settle down with us. But she reassures me by jumping on to my lap and kissing me fervently, then curling up into what I call my Beautiful Bundle of Susie. She is heavy now, surely her full adult weight though only seven months old. I dare not try to lift her from ground level – only from a chair or from the bed. But she is not keen on being lifted up, thank goodness, resembling Jock rather than Sheena in that respect, though she enjoys being hoisted on to my lap to get a peep out of one of the upstairs windows, intrigued at the familiar view seen from a different angle.

Her face is very striking, narrowing to a small black

----

muzzle. Her hair is dark grey tinged with fawn, dark speckled lines radiating from her eyes. These are brightly expressive, honey brown and emphasised with black velvet eye-liner. She has the distinctive "eye guards" of her breed, the tiny wisp of hair like a curving eyelash in front of each eye, just as Jock had. They must have evolved as a protection to shield the eyes from an enemy.

February 1st Gave her another worm pill to see if it would put a stop to her tail chasing. It does seem to have made a difference. She is less persistent with the habit and no longer shows signs of distress or seriously tries to bite her tail. She does a lot of other chewing, though. What was a full sized walking stick a few weeks ago is now little more than a foot long stump with a one-inch handle.

February 9th A big event – I took Susie to an obedience class for beginners, just to observe. It was all a bit overpowering. So many dogs, ranging from tiny Tim the Jack Russell, only four months old, to a hefty St. Bernard, all novices. And so much noise echoing round the Hall, dogs shouting at each other, handlers shouting to them to sit, and the instructor shouting to make herself heard. Susie had never seen so many dogs at once, even at the vet's surgery, and had never met so many kind and understanding people who welcomed her when she wriggled up to them wanting to make friends.

I sat with her on the sidelines, and she was rather restless, but every time the class was made to "sit" I made her sit too, and by the time the session was over she was fairly relaxed. The short drive there and back in the car was an experience too, as she hadn't been out in the streets at night until then. It so happened that just before she got in to the car to set out, and again as she jumped out when we got home, a black cat appeared. It may have been a sign of good luck, but on both occasions it caused an uproar that shattered the peace of Meadows Way and brought at least one resident to the door to see who was being murdered.

March 31st Susie has well and truly taken her place in the family and is now a highly intelligent ten-month-old teenager, fully grown physically but retaining her sense of puppy fun. She exercises herself and us with prolonged "ballie games" in the sitting room, retrieving long throws, catching and holding bouncers and short pitches with great dexterity. Having caught the ball she drops it to the ground and carefully nudges it back with one deft stroke of her nose to me or to Don. She will soon be as accurate as a putter on the green.

As a variation she will leap on to her chair with the ball in her mouth and then painstakingly push it off over the arm or front of the chair. She is delighted by her achievement if it bounces well, especially if it happens to roll over to us so that it can be lobbed back to her. She stands on her chair, eyes riveted on the ball, ears flattened with concentration, and catches it without moving.

She has invented a special exercise to develop her forearm muscles. Lying flat on her side on the floor in front of her chair she flails her front legs rhythmically against the chair, to the great detriment of the upholstery.

Even in wintry conditions she is happy to spend ages in the garden by herself, standing half-concealed under the cupressus tree in the far corner where the chain link fence is not covered by wooden boarding and she can watch the windows of the old peoples' home. If anyone appears at a window or passes in the garden of the home there is noisy barking. If a C.A.T. (do not even whisper the word) should

----

show itself all hell is let loose and she races madly up and down shouting her head off and has to be quietened to brought indoors to calm down.

She still goes through her nocturnal performance as a sprite of darkness, turning on the act the moment I call her to come in late at night. Prancing and pouncing she flits about over the lifeless frozen ground as if it were alive with magic. Unless I go out and threaten to whack her with a rolled up newspaper and spoil all the fun, it may take a full five minutes for me to break the spell and lure her indoors, my little witch, my Susiebell.

We are at winter's end now and the garden is a shambles. The lawn over which she presides with her mystical rites is pitted with small craters of her making, the lifeless grass trampled and muddy. The whole area is untidy with twigs she has bitten off, no sooner tidied away than fresh ones appear. The Eleagnus and the ivy on the wall are shorn of all their lower branches, the higher ones chewed off as far as she can reach, four feet or more from the ground. The mauled ends are attacked savagely at times. She will leap up and grab one of them, holding on like grim death and giving vent to blood-curdling squeals. With her hind legs dangling above the ground she looks like a man-eating Alsatian hanging onto its prey in a state of wild fury.

We wondered why she was behaving strangely last week, refusing her food, screwing up the old jersey in her basket into a tight ball, hiding in a nest beneath the canvas bed in the sun room and peering out at me while I did the washing up. Until I checked my diary and realised that it was nine weeks since she came into season for the first time in her life, and she was enacting the rituals of pregnancy.

Life is not going to be dull with Susie for company.

Black-Eyed Susie

May Susie's birthday is on May 27th. She is one year old this week, as late spring merges into early summer, the most exalted festal season, the very crowning of the year. Days still lengthening, warm days of hazy sunshine and showers, a sense of expectation in the air.

The birds are jubilant, rejoicing aloud from the earliest chorus before four in the morning to full evensong in the afterglow of sunset, well past nine o'clock. Sparrows chatter all day long from roofs and gutters and branches and there is a raucous screeching of starlings, relieved from time to time by lovely solos from blackbird and thrush.

Near my bedroom window there is a soft twittering from the house martins' nest that has been newly patched up and reoccupied for the first time for several years. Creamy pink clematis Montana cascades down over the high wall by the garage.

It is exactly seven years since I took Jessie to begin her new life in exile. The blackbird's evening song brings it all back, and I know again the heartache of parting and recall the long drive through bridal may blossom. And Sheena is gone too.

But Susie is bursting with happiness. The renewal of life and growth all around spells fresh excitement for her. Once again there are bizz-bizzes to chase – a bizz-bizz being any flying insect, from huge bumble bees to tiny fruit flies. Bluebottles are the best. Indoors she sits for ages watching a speck on the wall, ready to leap at it if it moves, and out in the garden she canters tirelessly round and round on the lookout for real or imaginary flying objects.

Not only is the air full of insects but everything in the garden is growing. The hydrangeas and other surviving perennials are in leaf again, giving cover for her as she wends her way along her private route at the back of the border.

107

She is delighted when it is warm enough to me to sit out of doors, and shows off her paces with redoubled energy.

The lawn is recovering from the ravages of winter, the craters camouflaged by the newly growing grass. But I have given away the geraniums that I had been carefully nurturing indoors through the winter. The narrow bed where they would have been planted out is on her much used jungle trail and they would not have stood a chance. It will be interesting to see whether the three sturdy tomatoes that I have planted, optimistically, close to the kitchen wall and protected by deeply sunk canes, will ever reach maturity.

Our latest Cairn child is a problem in some ways. Recently I have been using a choke chain when we go out for our daily walk, but so far there is little sign of improvement in her behaviour. It is like trying to cope with a horse that pulls. A walk with her is a stifled gallop.

I refuse to check her by yanking the lead fiercely in the approved manner, temporarily choking her into submission, preferring to use my voice and hands to make her pause to get her breath, so I suppose I should not be surprised that using the chain makes little difference. So far, anyway.

None of my other children was so difficult. Jock was perfectly docile on the lead. Perhaps because he was allowed so much freedom to wander at will by himself, so that he was not full of bottled up frustration as poor Susie seems to be.

Here in the heart of the town it would be unthinkable to let her roam free. There are too many potential hazards, from traffic, from other dogs, from cats that fascinate, just asking to be chased; and all around, a maze of streets in which she could get lost. She is not inclined to stay around, ready to come at my call, but can disappear at lightning speed if she has a mind to, Perhaps we tend to be over protective with

----

her, remembering Buffy's fate, but I would rather be safe than sorry.

Buffy, of course, had been trained to a very high standard of obedience and it was a joy to walk with her. The only time I ever took her into a show ring she won second prize for "best dog of any breed".

Sheena gave no trouble either, and I used to let her off the lead for much of the time when we were away from traffic. She seldom left my side, and if she did linger behind would always come trotting up to me when called.

As for Jessie, she learned by imitation, walking side by side with Sheena during her formative months. But Susie has no close doggy friends to set her an example. We must persevere and hope.

She still sleeps downstairs on a chair, or occasionally upstairs in the study next to my bedroom. Very early in the morning, at first light, there is a quick, soft flapping of ears as she shakes herself awake, and a few seconds later a little dark head appears round the edge of my open door. Half asleep, I stretch out a hand from under the quilt to greet her, and she jumps silently up on to her nest on the old cabin trunk and curls up to resume her sleep.

There is not a sound until the newspaper boy stuffs the papers through the letter box, causing Susie to rush headlong down the stairs with angry expletives, just as Sheena did in her younger days.

I am afraid our little Susiebell, so bright and beautiful, is not altogether ladylike. She is appallingly randy, and has always been so., When I pull the papers in through the letter box, or stoop to pick up the letters from the door mat, she goes into a frenzy, standing on her hind legs and grabbing my arm or leg in a vice-like grip. Unaccountably, she does not even attempt such behaviour with Don, though she sometimes tries it on with a visitor. I disengage myself and discourage her firmly but gently, telling her she must not hug her mummy so hard. It is very difficult to be cross with her.

Don calls her Superdog, and we love her dearly.

"Perhaps", he said when she first arrived, "she is Sheena come back to us." I think not, though I sometimes wonder if she is Jock re-embodied in female form, so strongly is she endowed with masculine energies.

August 16th The first really hot but fresh and non-humid day for over a month, following excessively rainy and chilly weather. Cloudless deep blue sky. House martins sweeping in large insect-hunting flocks, crying out with incessant little tissicks as they fly.

A wood pigeon has been calling, that lovely, lazy, settled sound of summer, gentle and contented. It is so hot that the leaves of the runner beans, now seven feet high against the wall, are drooping with dehydration. Hopefully it will help to ripen the tomatoes. The hydrangea blossoms are enormous after the wet season.

September 19th Suddenly the house martins have vanished. Silence from the nest near my window. No more of that soft twittering, the happy sound I have grown used to hearing from soon after daybreak until late into the night. No more busy parent birds swooping around and in and out of the nest bearing food for the young. Not a twitter from the TV aerial.

Susie's new game of swallow-tailing is over when it had scarcely begun. She learned it only two weeks ago. I have recently summoned the courage to let her run free in the playing field, first making sure that the whole area is free of other dogs, and keeping a constant lookout, like a security man guarding a celebrity.

The best time is soon after one o'clock, when most people and their dogs are indoors. Suddenly one day at such a time she became aware of those low-flying insect-seeking house martins, and the game was on. She selects her target and takes off like a bullet, racing with incredible speed round and round following the flight path, like a greyhound after a hare. She goes almost berserk, reaching such a pitch of excitement that she is completely deaf to my calls.

I can put the brake on by moving into the middle of the field and thereby keeping the birds away, but she merely stands stock still, panting, with tongue hanging, ears cocked, waiting for her quarry to reappear. Only exhaustion finally brings the game to a halt, and she flops down on the turf, and then if I move very quickly I may be lucky enough to catch her. It's a glorious game. Until today. When I let her off the lead she stood looking around expectantly, staring upwards for her quarry, but they did not appear. No more house martins. We are bereft. The happy, happy birds have gone; only the robin is singing now. It is less than four months since they gladdened us by their arrival. The old nest was only patched up and occupied at the beginning of June. So short a visit.

September 21st We were fooled – they have not all gone. The nest was occupied overnight. Several times during the hours of darkness I heard that heart-stopping sound, a tiny twitter of conversation, and this morning I caught sight of several flying around near the house.

October 18th The nest is still occupied at night, in spite of the most disastrous gale since 1703. It occurred in the early hours of October 16th.

We became aware that something out of the ordinary was happening when we were woken by the sound of the raging wind. It was obviously no ordinary gale. Instead of intermittent gusts of wind there was an almost continuous tearing roar, wavering only slightly in intensity. At about six am we discovered that the lights were not working; there had been a power failure, not too surprisingly.

Presently we saw some of the neighbours gathered in the road outside pointing apparently at the roofs of their houses. At first we could not see what was wrong, but in fact most of the ridge tiles of the west-facing gables had been torn off. I went out soon afterwards and discovered just round the corner large branches of trees strewn across the road. Near the market place a huge sycamore was lying across the street, completely blocking it. People were standing about in the street and talking, unable to get to work because the roads out of town were blocked; the interiors of the shops were in darkness, electrically operated tills out of action.

Right across the breadth of southern England roads and railways were blocked, buildings damaged, cars crushed or blown away, whole forests pillaged. Electricity was cut off and telegraph wires were down, so we had to rely on transistor radios for news of what was going on. Or not going on. But the house martins' nest is on the north-facing wall of the house so that it escaped the full force of the wind, and the tiny occupants were unharmed. In the garden only the cupressus tree in the far corner, partly sheltered by the ten foot brick wall, was affected. It stands permanently listing to the east like the leaning tower of Pisa, a memorial to that epochal gale.

October 20th They've really gone. Lucky birds, off on their way to Africa. How we envy them. With no swallows to chase, Susie does less racing. Instead, when let off the lead in the playing field, she will give a demonstration of the mole dance. It always amuses the passers by. She leaps about with a prancing action, all four feet in the air at once, like a Lippizaner stallion, and pretends to pounce on her imaginary prey, nose to the ground and tearing out divots of turf with her teeth. This may be kept up for five minutes or more with great concentration and busyness. Somewhere, sometime in the past, her forbears must have been trained to catch moles.

I have now made a very useful discovery. She loves the aniseed flavour of the little coloured chew sticks sold in pet food shops, in fact she is quite crazy about them. I have only to take a small piece out of my pocket and tempt her with it when it is time for her to come on the lead again, and she gobbles it up ravenously, sometimes coming up to me unbidden and demanding it quite forcefully. It is a very useful tool, solving one of my big problems. Except, however, when there is something more distracting around, such as another dog or a cat. Then it may be really difficult to catch her.

October 26th There was frantic barking in the garden at 4.15. It was overcast and the light beginning to fade, the clocks having just been put back to winter time. Susie had found a hedgehog in the narrow bed under the kitchen window - actually inside her garden! She was quite furious. I dragged her indoors and went outside with a large cardboard box. Poor frightened Horace was trying to burrow under the turf at the edge of the bed. I picked him up with gloved hands, put him gently in the box and presented him to our next door neighbours. They gladly agreed to let him out in their back garden from whence there is apparently a hedgehog trail leading into the garden of the old peoples' home, which seems to be a sanctuary for beast as well as man.

May 1988 To mate or not to mate? Susie, mature and beautiful, was due to come into season around the time of her second birthday, May 29th. But I was taken by surprise in the middle of the month when she showed the first signs, and became more nervy and excitable than usual.

There seems to be a dearth of male Cairns in this part of the world. However, after a few phone calls I located one who was ready and willing and in due course, the date being auspicious, we went to call on him.

But Toby when introduced wasn't particularly interested, and Susie, though quite animated at first encounter, said primly that he wasn't her type anyway, so there. We went back a few days later, but the joint verdict was the same.

Then we heard about Charlie. Charlie was young, well-bred and handsome and they got on very well together, uproarious games alternating with quiet tête-á-têtes on two extended visits. They made a lovely pair and Charlie tried most gallantly to play his part, but in spite of all our encouragement they remained "just good friends". There could be no question of forcing Susie into submission.

June 15th Today I disposed of the last remains of dear Dolly, Sheena's lifelong familiar, reduced now to a bald rubber skull whose pretty face had been chewed almost out of recognition by Susie. It is a miracle that she has survived the abuse for so long. Poor Dolly. She came with Sheena when she first arrived on our doorstep fifteen years ago, wrapped in a transparent plastic bag, and even then she was literally only a pretty face with a shock of reddish hair but no torso. In Sheena's care she survived alternate bouts of severe treatment, carried in her mouth as she charged up and down the sitting room with ferocious growls, and long sessions of heavy maternal licking. Whereas Susie treated her as if she were vermin, a rat that must be dispatched by vicious shaking and bashing on the ground.

June 23rd The essence of summer. Really hot when the sun comes out, very warm when cloudy. Elderberry blossom in full creamy bloom, rosebuds nearly open. Blackbirds and thrushes singing intermittently, in glorious ringing tones. One repeats quite distinctly: "You *lucky* little boy!" Sparrows chirping loudly all the time, a collared dove calling. The first week of Wimbledon, strawberries and cream. The french window open to the garden all day, so that Susie can come and go freely, or sit in the opening and enjoy the slight draught.

This is what we dream about all through the dark, cold days of the year.

June 25th Four weeks since her romp with Charlie. Is she or isn't she? I don't think it's possible, but haven't quite given up hope – this morning for the third time she was slightly sick at breakfast time.

July 1st. Twice lately Susie has announced with wild shrieks from the garden that she has seen a hedgehog, and each time when I have gone out to look, at her insistence, over the fence to the garden beyond, there, creeping away in broad daylight has been a full-grown specimen. She almost bursts with rage and excitement. When ordered to be quiet she comes away only with the utmost reluctance, leaping up and grabbing the

Eleagnus with screams of frustration.

It is a pity that her strong hunting instincts have to be suppressed. She would love to get at a hedgehog, to kill a rat or chase and if possible exterminate the black cat, and also, I suspect, the miniature Yorkies and other toy dogs who sometimes pass our way. I wish there were wide moors where she could roam freely and hunt, and dig for prey and play with others of her kind.

July 21st She has reverted to her old habit of creeping softly up the stairs in the morning as soon as she hears us stir – or when she reckons it is time we did wake up – and leaping full tilt on to my bed before I can stop her. The one time I shouted "No!" and prevented her from jumping up she was so upset and overcome that she retreated downstairs again, and looked up nervously when I went down later, her feelings badly hurt.

July 28th Today should have been delivery date, but nothing has happened. I have preserved an open mind up to the very last minute, remembering how Sheena fooled even the vet and then produced a puppy. Susie has been very nervy and lost her appetite, and has been searching all over the house for suitable hiding places, scrabbling about in the old dog basket, a place she usually avoids. It is amazing that the natural inbuilt cycle of gestation is so accurately timed and instinct so strong, even in the absence of pregnancy.

July 30th Hedgehogs again. Summoned by unusually excited barking to the corner where the tall cupressus stands, I looked over the fence just in time to see a small half-grown hedgehog staggering away amongst the weeds of the uncultivated plot beyond. Some six or seven feet away he

----

collapsed and rolled up. I took Susie indoors.

A little later I noticed that she was staring intently through the french window. There, unbelievably, in the middle of the lawn was the rounded tawny form of another young hedgehog. A rescue operation was necessary.

I found a large cardboard box, put on my gardening gloves, and leaving Susie indoors gently picked up the prickly little body. Susie watched suspiciously as I carried him through the house and out of the front door. I handed him over to our kind neighbour who was by now getting used to helping in such odd emergencies and was happy to set the youngster free in her garden. His brother (or sister) remained curled up beyond the fence, though, and as the day wore on and he did not move it seemed that he must be injured. But there was nothing I could do.

July 31st Little Hedgie was still lying there this morning. Watching intently it was just possible to make out that he was still breathing, but the sight of a bluebottle fly buzzing round suggested that there was blood about.

The sun blazed down. I racked my brains to try and think of some way to help. At intervals during the morning I went to look at him. The place was deserted. Once I saw him take a deep breath, the little body heaving almost imperceptibly. It was very hot – he must be thirsty. I soaked some small pieces of bread in milk and threw them very carefully so that they landed softly near him. But there was no reaction; he was beyond fear now. I waited and watched, but there was no more movement.

My first reaction was one of relief. At last he was out of pain. But the sadness was overpowering. Even the death of a hedgehog is diminishing.

I think he must have been trying to follow his brother, who

117

----

had in some mysterious way managed to circumnavigate the fence, and possibly his nose or part of his body may have been stuck in the fence when Susie pounced on him and injured him. Thus he would have been unable to follow the natural reaction to danger by curling up at once into a spiny ball to protect himself. Afterwards he had only just been able to stagger a few paces away from the fence before collapsing, fatally injured.

Every day I went to the fence and looked at his pathetic remains lying undisturbed until the scavengers of the soil, undetected, had done their work and all that remained was a little flattened tawny circle gradually covered by grass and groundsel.

It served as a warning to his brother and any other adventurous relatives to keep well away from the fence in future as long as Susie held sway.

August 2nd Susie's particular bête noir, Black Pussy, is away while his family is on holiday, removing what is usually a source of the greatest annoyance and frustration. It so infuriates her to see him sunning himself in full view on the pavement or on the lawn opposite, as if to taunt her, or curled up on the roof tiles beside the dormer windows of his home.

But today she flushed out another cat that was lurking in Black Pussy's territory and chased it smartly up a cherry tree. It took me ages to catch her. Round and round she circled while the cat glowered down at her from the branches. She can be as slippery as an eel if she has a mind to evade capture.

However shocking it may sound to the pundits, and however maddening she can be at times like this, though, I would never try and break her spirit and force her into submission, or punish her for disobedience. It is not in her nature to act like a mechanical robot, to sit down the moment she is told or to come the very instant she is called. She is by no means the boss, but she is a person with an independent spirit. And she is quicker to obey than she used to be. She will emerge <u>almost</u> instantaneously from the shadows in the garden when I summon her at night unless her attention is distracted by something riveting, like a passing cat, or one of the residents looking out of a window at her. Which is of course excusable.

August 8th This morning I had been sitting in the garden in the warm sunshine observing the activity of a busy little speckled thrush. It would alight at intervals on the high brick wall opposite my place in the sun, sharply outlined against the bright sky. Often when it alighted it was possible to distinguish a tiny scrap held in its beak, and it would perch stock still for a few seconds to make sure the coast was clear.

Meantime, from the hidden recesses of the cupressus tree came an insistent hungry cheeping. The instant the parent bird flitted into the branches with its offering, the chirping ceased.

All the morning, whether I sat outside or came indoors to potter in the kitchen the loud persistent cheeping continued in the background, with only short intervals of satiety. Susie was well aware of it, and was keeping an eye on the situation.

Suddenly while I was sitting there a small fluffy object launched itself from the shady depths of the tree and fluttered unsteadily towards the tall runner beans growing against the wall, landing amongst the upper leaves. Susie was there instantly, alert and crouching ready to spring. I dragged her indoors protesting strongly, and made her stay inside the house until after lunch. Eventually, thinking that the young bird had had ample time to retreat to its nest or to some other safe place, I opened the french window again; it was normally left open all day in such weather. The loud cheep-cheeping had been resumed – and Susie's interest was undiminished.

It was not long before the dreaded but unavoidable moment came. I was in the kitchen doing the washing up when there was a sudden wild, anguished outburst of the thrush's danger call. The parent bird was beside herself.

And there on the lawn was Susie with the young fledgling in her mouth. She carried the limp body indoors and deposited it on the sitting room carpet. The garden was suddenly quiet. No more cheeping from the cupressus tree, no more alarm calls.

True to her breeding, Susie is an inveterate killer. You have to see the power and energy with which she dispatches a three-foot long sapling to appreciate the strength of the instinct within her. She rages and growls and shakes it mercilessly, baring her large tiger teeth and banging it on the ground, just as she used to do with her toy rattle when she was a puppy, leaving her thick mane fluffed up. Just the treatment she would like to mete out to the black cat.

But her anger soon subsides – another kill achieved, all part of the day's work to her. Angry growling is soon replaced by playful muttering, as she lies on her back still grasping the stick in her teeth, no longer a victim but a plaything, wriggling and twisting her body so that the end of the stick gets entangled with her hind legs.

She talks to us a lot, and sometimes to herself. Curled up in her armchair she will suddenly make a little grunting comment addressed to no one in particular, and if I answer

---

her she looks quite surprised. She talks far more than the other dogs used to. Even, to my annoyance, when she has settled on my bed in the early morning and I, having been woken by her unceremonious landing on top of my legs, am trying to get a little more sleep.

August 22nd 1988. A large flock of perhaps thirty or forty house martins were sunning themselves on the south facing roof of the house this morning, and a group of them bunched on the TV aerial. It was quite impossible to count them as they were constantly taking off and landing again, chattering incessantly in their little squeaky voices and behaving generally like a crowd of excited children anticipating a treat.

Suddenly Susie became aware of them. She does not normally take any notice of the martins when she is in the garden because they are outside her line of vision as they swoop high overhead; the garden is too small for them to enter our own confined airspace. But now she noticed them thronging the roof, and stood surveying them with an air of hostility, an antipathy which must have been conveyed to them, even at roof-top height, for with one accord the whole flock rose and vanished with a quick whoosh of wings. Then a few returned, and in a few minutes the whole roof was covered again with chattering birds, until the sun went in and they were gone once more, almost soundlessly. A training exercise no doubt, in preparation for the incredible marathon flight to come.

Throughout September there were bursts of great activity. Flocks of martins appeared out of the blue and swooped round and round in front of the house chirping excitedly, repeatedly zooming up to the nest under the eaves and away again, then disappearing en masse. With each great flurry they seemed to be saluting their summertime haunts, saying goodbye; or perhaps more importantly they were impressing on their memory the exact location of the nest so that they could return unerringly next season. One bird at a time would hover fluttering for a split second within a few inches of the entrance to the little round home, then swoop away; just occasionally one would alight and enter the nest. Some mornings the ritual took place as early as 8 am, sometimes late in the day.

September 30th 1988. A perfect autumn day. After the first touch of frost in the night, a cloudless sky and warm sunshine. Ideal for a game of swallow-tailing, we thought, Susie and I. We went to the playing field and I let her off the lead. We waited. She stood stock still gazing around in all directions, ears pricked, tense with anticipation. But nothing happened. No tiny specks swooped down from the sky skimming the air for insects. There was none of the familiar twittering, no sound of any birds. In the garden at home just the tik-tik of the robin's territorial call. They had all gone.

Next morning I looked out of the bedroom window to see just two little martins perched on a TV aerial. They sat quietly together for a long time, preening themselves and warming their tiny bodies in the sun. Wondering, perhaps, where everyone else had gone. I hope they survived the journey to Africa.

House martins, hedgehogs, cats, thrushes and other birds, not to mention other dogs, all play a part in Susie's life, as do the imaginary moles that she pretends to hunt when she performs her mole dance n the playing field, and the bizz-bizzes that animate the air in summertime.

Among the joyous encounters that highlight her days are the meetings with Harvey, Margie's smooth-coated merle collie who was with us on the memorable occasion when we went to find Susie and brought her home as a twelve-week old puppy. He is a long-suffering playmate, more than twice her size, her very most favourite friend. He will sit patiently while she dances round him, and when they are both let out together in the garden he will race round in circles, to be intercepted by Susie tearing round in the opposite direction and pretending to snap at him when they collide. They have a very special relationship, embracing over and over again when they meet and exchanging licky kisses, even on occasion carrying out the ritual chewing and exchange of bones as Jock and Buffy did. Once we found them late at night facing each other across Margie's sitting room, Susie on an armchair, Harvey on the settee, comfortably settled down for a romantic night together (they hoped).

She no longer demands long, tireless ballie games. Sometimes she will present us with the ball, but loses interest after a couple of catches. Her speciality nowadays, if one of us happens to go upstairs, is to follow and place the ball carefully on the landing near the top step. She then creeps quietly down to the hall and crouches expectantly. The game is to topple the ball, with the toe, gently over the top step so that it appears to move of its own accord and bounces down from step to step to be caught in mid air at the final bounce with enormous satisfaction.

I will close the story of my cairn children with a word portrait of Susie, now three years old.

It is evening and she is dozing in her big armchair, snuggled up against her own small shabby cushion, utterly relaxed and at peace. Her dark ears fringed with curving wisps of silky hair are set close together, her eyes half closed, and just visible is the tiniest tip of pink tongue.

Susie at her most beguiling and sweet, fully aware that in such a mood and in such a posture she is quite irresistible. So that I am compelled to leave my chair and go and crouch on the floor beside her and run my fingers through her thick brindled coat. She acknowledges this homage with a gentle lick of my hand, and lies back, slightly stretching her hind legs, to expose her pink tummy with its silken underwear, and I tell her that she is the most beautiful person in all the world.

POSTSCRIPT

Don (or Scrim as he was generally known) died in 1993, his body racked by asthma. He had survived many years of valiant struggle against addiction with unfailing cheerfulness.

He surprised himself and everybody else by reaching his seventy-second birthday, and declared that having got that far he was going to live to be eighty even if it killed him.

Seven days later the trumpets sounded for him on the other side.

So no more is it "we three" in the family, but just the two of us. Susie and I look after each other.